W9-AGK-895

First Science Experiments

with Nature, Senses, Weather & Machines

First Science Experiments

with Nature, Senses, Weather & Machines

by Shar Levine and Leslie Johnstone
illustrations by Steve Harpster

Main Street
A division of Sterling Publishing Co., Inc.
New York

Library of Congress Cataloging-in-Publication Data Available

2   4   6   8   10   9   7   5   3   1

Published by Sterling Publishing Co., Inc.
387 Park Avenue South, New York, NY 10016
© 2005 by Sterling Publishing Co., Inc.

This book is comprised of materials from the following Sterling Publishing Co., Inc. titles:
Nifty Nature © 2004 by Shar Levine and Leslie Johnstone
Wonderful Weather © 2003 by Shar Levine and Leslie Johnstone
Mighty Machines © 2004 by Shar Levine and Leslie Johnstone
Super Senses © 2003 by Shar Levine and Leslie Johnstone

Printed in China
All rights reserved

Sterling ISBN 1-4027-2922-7

For information about custom editions, special sales, premium and
corporate purchases, please contact Sterling Special Sales
Department at 800-805-5489 or specialsales@sterlingpub.com.

Contents

Note to Parents and Teachers

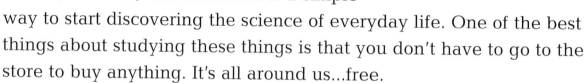

This book is designed to answer very basic questions young children have about science. Kids are curious about the world around them, and looking at nature, senses, weather, and machines is a simple way to start discovering the science of everyday life. One of the best things about studying these things is that you don't have to go to the store to buy anything. It's all around us...free.

Obviously we can't explain all the mysteries of science, but we can start you and your child on the road to discovery. Along the way you may be surprised to learn something new, too. If your child wants to know more about a specific topic, you can visit the library to find a book on the subject. Surf the Internet with your child and research the question using a search engine where you can type in your question and be directed to a number of sites that may provide answers. Make a list or diary of your child's questions and work with your child to find the answers. Just think of the things you may discover together!

Safety First: These activities are designed to be as safe and simple as possible. Some adult supervision is suggested with small children, especially when performing experiments outdoors. Please read the **Be Safe** checklist with your child before starting any of the activities.

Be Safe

DO

- ✔ Before starting, ask an adult for permission to do the experiment.
- ✔ Read through each experiment with an adult first.
- ✔ If you have allergies or asthma, let a parent decide which experiments you can safely do.
- ✔ Have an adult handle anything that is sharp or made of glass.
- ✔ Keep babies and pets away from experiments and supplies.
- ✔ Wash your hands when you are finished.
- ✔ Keep your work area clean. Wipe up spills right away.
- ✔ Tell an adult right away if you or anyone else gets hurt!

DON'T

- ✔ Don't put any part of these experiments in your mouth.
- ✔ Never look directly at the sun or go out without a hat, sunscreen, and insect repellant.
- ✔ Never touch or harm spiders, stinging insects, or snakes.
- ✔ Never go out during a thunderstorm or dangerous windstorm.
- ✔ Don't experiment with or take apart any object before you get an adult's permission.
- ✔ Never put a screwdriver on anything that plugs into the wall and never put anything made of metal into a wall outlet.

NIFTY NATURE

Nature

Look out a window and what do you see? No matter where you are, you can see some part of nature. The beauty of the natural world is all around you, from the clouds in the sky to the dirt on the ground, and everywhere in between. See that tiny ant scurrying across the porch? Don't crush it! Take a moment instead to watch where it's going and what it's doing.

Do you think of science as rocket ships and test tubes, chemicals and computers? Well, there's science in nature, too. Have you ever wondered why leaves change color in the fall or ants march in a line?

This chapter may help explain some of life's little mysteries. It will help you begin to see that there's more to science than meets the eye.

Plants, for instance, are really important to every living thing. Close your eyes and imagine the world without plants. Instead of a place rich with life and color, earth would be a sandy desert. All living things would die because they would have nothing to eat. Even rivers and lakes would die. In the first section, you will begin to see how wonderful plants really are.

Did You Know?

When you buy bananas in the grocery store, you generally choose unripe or green ones. After a few days on the counter, the bananas turn a deep yellow, much as leaves do in the fall in some places, and for the same reason (see page 16). Then they're ready to eat.

Plants

To begin to see the wonder of plants, let's first take a look at seeds. The variety of their shapes and sizes alone is amazing. Plants spread their seeds in many ways. Some, like maple trees, have seeds with special shapes that let them hitch a ride on a breeze to their new home. Other seeds have sharp bristles that attach to animal fur and get carried to new places. Still others, like those of apples and pears, get eaten with their fruit by passing animals. The seeds pass right through the animals and become part of a rich fertilizer.

Fruit trees like papaya have yet another way to spread their seeds: the fruit stays on the tree, but the bottom gets really soft and the seeds just drop out of the rotting fruit.

In some ways, it would be nice if fruit didn't have seeds. In fact, for many years, there have been seedless oranges and grapes in the grocery store...even seedless watermelons. But if these fruit don't have seeds, how do they start new plants? Scientists have ways of creating fruit that nature never dreamed of. With seedless fruit, shoots or buds from the original plant are rooted or **grafted** onto similar growing plants, where they grow and mature (see bolded words in Glossary, pages 185–186).

Look at the fruits and vegetables you eat. Can you see the seeds?

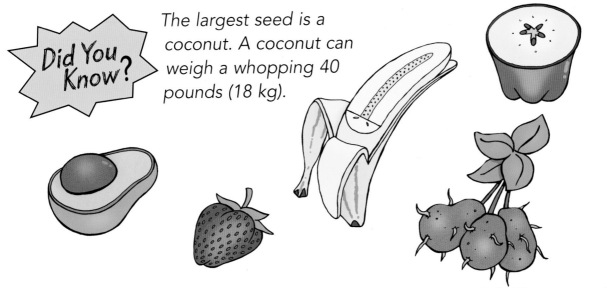

Did You Know?

The largest seed is a coconut. A coconut can weigh a whopping 40 pounds (18 kg).

When you work with plants, remember to be careful. If you want just a leaf or a flower, don't pull the whole plant up by the roots. Have an adult help you cut or pick what you need. Don't raid a park or your neighbor's garden. Ask for permission first. And if you're not sure if a plant is safe to touch, ask an adult.

why do leaves change color

Where the weather is always warm, the trees may be green all year round. But where the summers are warm and the weather cools suddenly in the autumn, the leaves often turn brilliant shades of red, orange, and yellow. Exactly why does this happen?

You need

* coffee filter
* scissors
* leaf from a tree or plant
* spoon
* tape
* rubbing alcohol
* lidded glass jar, 6 inches (15 cm) tall

Do this

1 From the coffee filter, cut a strip 6 inches (15 cm) x 1 inch (2.5 cm). Place the leaf—either side up—on top of the coffee filter strip, 1 inch (2.5 cm) from the end.

2 Rub the leaf with the spoon handle to make a green line or streak across the narrow side of the strip.

3 Tape the end of the strip farther from the streak to the inside of the jar lid.

4 Have an adult pour ¹/₄ cup (40 mL) of rubbing alcohol into the jar to cover the bottom. Lower the strip into the alcohol and close the lid on the jar. Watch the strip for several minutes. What do you see?

5 Have an adult take the strip out of the jar and let it dry.

What happened?

As the alcohol moved up the filter strip, it passed through the green streak of pigment and took it along for the ride. This green pigment is chlorophyll. Made up of tiny particles called **molecules**, it makes leaves green and helps them use sunlight to grow. Bigger molecules travel more slowly than smaller ones. Eventually they separate on the strip, so you see different bands of color.

The truth is that leaves don't really change color; they just lose chlorophyll. When it gets very cold in the fall, the leaves die and their chlorophyll breaks down. Then we see other pigments left behind in the leaves.

How do plants get water ?

When you're thirsty, you can go to the fridge for a juice box or just get some water from the tap. But plants don't have things like electricity, plumbing, and appliances. So what do they do?

You need

- leaf
- water
- small plastic bottle
- modeling clay
- drinking straws
- friend or mirror
- magnifying glass (optional)

Do this

1. Pluck a leaf from a tree or plant, leaving a long stem.

2. Fill a small bottle (like that used for bottled water) to 1 inch (2.5 cm) from the top with tap water.

3. Wrap a flattened piece of modeling clay around the top of the bottle. Poke the stem of the plant through the clay, making sure it touches the water.

4 Push the straw through a small hole in the clay; stop it above the water. Be sure not to get clay in the straw. Seal the clay around the straw and the leaf stem.

5 Have a friend watch the leaf as you use the straw to suck out the air in the bottle. Then put in a new straw and watch what happens as your friend sucks out the air through the straw.

6 Try this with different kinds of leaves. Does the size of the leaf make a difference?

What happened?

Leaves are specially designed to help plants breathe and drink. They take in air and water in much the same way you used the straw. If you look at the underside of a leaf with a magnifying glass, you may see tiny holes, or **stomata**. These are the openings to long tubes inside the plant stem. When you sucked the air out of the sealed bottle, the leaf replaced it by drawing air in from the outside. You can see this in the bubbles released out the cut end of the stem. Just like you, plants can't live without air.

Can plants move

If you have a cat or a dog, you may have seen it curl up to sleep in a warm, sunny spot. As the sun moves, your pet may move too, so it can keep basking in the rays. But did you know that plants enjoy sunlight just as much as animals do?

You need
- potted flowering plant
- sunny window

Do this

1. In the morning, turn the pot so that the plant's flowers or leaves are facing the inside of the room, away from the light.

2. Throughout the day, check which way the flowers and leaves are facing. Do they follow the movement of the sun?

3 If it is summer, watch the flower heads in the garden. Do they move, too?

What happened?

The leaves and flowers turned to follow the sun. The sun's stronger light on one side of the stem activated chemicals in the plant that made one side grow faster than the other. This made the stem bend, tilting the leaves and flowers toward the sun. The word for this growth response to sunlight is phototropism, *photo* referring to light, and *tropism* referring to turning or curving.

Did You Know?

Here's another new word for you: nyctitropism. How does this relate to what you just learned? You found that in daylight, plants move to follow the sun. Well, at night, just like you, the leaves and flower petals of the plant come to rest in a neutral position. The word to describe this is— you guessed it—nyctitropism.

Wildlife

When you think of wildlife, big furry things like bears or lions may come to mind. But where would the average kid find wild creatures? A visit to a park, a forest, even your own backyard may bring a close encounter with beasts of many kinds.

In this section, you will start to see the value of even the smallest of living things. The most important thing is that they remain alive and unharmed after your meeting. Don't bother the bugs, worms, or birds you observe. Be very careful— getting too up close and personal with even little wild things has its hazards. Be sure to keep a safe distance from wasps, bees, and other stinging insects. Even tiny ants can band together and bite you.

You may find that some animals are awfully hard to see. To fool your eyes and keep you away, and to keep certain birds and other insects from seeing them at all, these animals use **camouflage**. Their shape and color help them hide. Some may look like leaves or twigs on the plants where they live. There are insects that are mimics: they look like other insects that taste bad to birds, so the birds leave them alone. Still other animals blend into their surroundings, as a white coat blends into a snowy background. And a green **algae** that grows in certain sloths' hair makes them the same color as the trees they live in.

Did You Know?

There's an insect in England that you might say has changed its spots over time. The Peppered Moth comes in two colors, light gray and dark gray. The light gray ones were much more common than the dark ones in the 1800s: the dark variety was easy for birds to see against the light-colored tree trunks, and they were eaten. As industrial development polluted the air and darkened the tree bark, the lighter moths' camouflage became ineffective, so they were more easily seen and eaten by birds. This meant that more dark moths survived. However, over the years, the air became cleaner and the color advantage shifted again. Once again, there are fewer dark gray moths.

Why do ladybugs have spots ?

If you don't really like the thought of a beetle on your body, you're not alone. But how about a ladybug? That's not so bad. Ladybugs are nice and harmless. They'll just walk on your body until it's time to fly away home. Let's take a closer look at ladybugs. **NOTE**: Be very gentle with this delicate bug. Do not pick it up between your fingers, hold its wings, or squish it.

You need
* ladybug
* magnifying glass

Do this

1 Find a ladybug on a tree, leaf, or vegetable. Hold your finger out for the bug to walk onto or use a leaf to scoop it up.

2 Take a closer look at your new friend with a magnifying glass. Can you find its head? Its mouth? How many legs does the ladybug have? Do you see the tips of the ladybug's wings sticking out under its spotted wing cases?

3 Place the bug on your palm and slowly turn your palm down. The bug will walk to the edge. Can you feel its tiny feet?

4 With the ladybug on a flat surface, flip it onto its back with your fingertip. Don't worry—this isn't harmful, like flipping a turtle. Watch how the bug turns itself over.

What happened?

Ladybugs are a kind of beetle and there are over 4,000 different kinds of them—about 400 in the United States alone. And ladybugs don't all look alike. Some have red wing covers, some, orange or yellow, with any number of dots, or even stripes!

Those marks are a ladybug's shield against hungry birds. You can't tell, but ladybugs smell terrible and taste even worse. A bird will eat a ladybug only once and avoid bugs with similar markings forever after.

Ladybugs are a farmer's friend: they eat other insects that destroy crops, so no pesticides are needed when they're around. And ladybugs love to eat—each one can devour over 100 aphids a day!

why do ants march in a line ?

You may know the song that starts, "The ants go marching one by one, hurrah, hurrah...." Your parents may even have sung it when they were kids. This raises the question: why do ants go marching in a line? Let's find out. **NOTE**: Don't get too close to an ants' nest. If the colony feels threatened, it may try to attack YOU!

You need

- ants
- sugar
- fruit or small piece of candy
- book
- old CD

Do this

1. Watch your sidewalk or garden for a line of ants. If you can't find one, place a little sugar on the sidewalk. Ants will quickly find the food.

2. Watch the ants. Are they carrying any food?

3. Place an object such as a book or a CD in the ants' path, being careful not to squish any of the ants. What happens when they discover their path is blocked?

4. Once the ants are settled into their new path, replace the object with another one. What do the ants do this time?

5. Remove the object. Gently blow on an ant so it goes off the path. What does the ant do now?

6. Place a small piece of candy or fruit on the sidewalk. Watch how the ants get the food back to their nest.

What happened?

Ants are pretty smart for their size. They always seek the shortest route from their food to the nest. You saw that even when an obstacle is put in their path, ants find their way again. You can't see it or smell it, but ants leave a trail of chemicals called **pheromones** that guides other ants. Each ant follows the scent of the ants that went before it. When something gets in the ant's way, it finds a new way. Soon, all the insects find the newer, shorter path and stop using the old long one.

Are butterflies just pretty moths

Butterflies are beautiful. Their delicate wings bear rich designs in colors ranging from deep metallic blue to palest yellow. If you'd like to know more about them, simply watching is a great way to learn.

You need
* adult helper
* your own yard or neighborhood, a public park or gardening space, or an indoor butterfly garden

Do this

1 Have an adult go with you to one of the places mentioned above and spend some time among the flowering plants. Try to find a local museum or garden that is holding an exhibit featuring butterflies flying free within a controlled environment.

2 Watch the plants for signs of butterflies and moths. Do not disturb them.

3 Draw pictures of some of the butterflies and moths you see.

What happened?

You got a good look at both moths and butterflies. Here's a foolproof way to tell the difference between them: when the insect lands, take a close look at its wings. If they are folded up and held together above the insect's body, it's a butterfly. A moth's wings fold down and over its body. In addition, the antennae of a butterfly resemble upside down baseball bats, while the moth's antennae look like feathers.

These insects have four stages of life, in some of which you might not even recognize them. They start as eggs and grow into **caterpillars**, little wiggly wormlike forms. Then they create **cocoons**, small hard shells in which to wait until they become butterflies and moths. Did you see any cocoons?

Did You Know? *The largest butterfly is found in Papua, New Guinea. The Queen Alexandra's Birdwing has a wingspan that can exceed 11 inches (28 cm)!*

Water

If you were to see Earth from space—or just look at a globe—you'd see that most of the planet is covered by water. And this water doesn't just stay put. It goes through a cycle. No, not like a bike, silly.

A cycle describes the recurring changes that water is continually undergoing. In a process called **evaporation**, it is changed by the sun's heat from water in the ocean to a gas or **vapor**. Heat carries the water vapor up into the sky, where it changes again by the process of **condensation**: it cools and joins other water molecules to form clouds. You've seen that dark, stormy clouds drop rain and snow. The drops and flakes fall from the sky, showering trees and towns, people and wildlife. The water that is not absorbed runs off into rivers, lakes, and oceans, and, yes...the whole thing starts again.

"The Rime of the Ancient Mariner" is a poem about a sailor who is stranded at sea and dying of thirst. "Water, water everywhere, Nor any drop to drink," he cries. If you have ever been in the ocean, you surely know that the water is very salty. The more you drink, the thirstier you become. How did the oceans get to be so salty anyway?

When water falls from the sky as rain or snow, some of it runs off into streams and rivers. As it flows, the water picks up mineral salts in the ground. The water finds its way back to the ocean, where a good portion of it evaporates, leaving behind the salt. Your body has no way to get rid of the extra salt in seawater. In fact, if you try to drink it, it will just make you more thirsty.

Scientists have developed ways to extract the salt from seawater, using the natural processes of evaporation and condensation, so that people can drink it. But some seabirds have organs above their eyes that remove the salt from  seawater, enabling the birds to drink salty water. The albatross, the bird featured in "The Rime of the Ancient Mariner," didn't have the sailor's problem. This bird can drink seawater because it has its own salt remover right on its face.

How can you make water cleaner

If your hands are dirty, you can use soap and water to clean up before you dig into dinner. But what happens when your water is dirty? You can't use soap and water to make water clean. In many places, there isn't enough clean or unpolluted water for people to drink. So what do they do?

You need

- water
- grass
- sand
- coffee filter
- pebbles
- plastic jars
- adult helper
- dirt
- leaves
- large plastic soda pop bottle
- crushed piece of charcoal (without lighter fluid)

Do this

1 Mix dirt, grass, leaves, and pebbles in a jar and add lots of water. Swirl the mixture around in the jar. There should be enough water for the mess to swirl freely.

2 Have an adult cut the top ¹/₄ off a plastic pop bottle. This top is the holder for your coffee filter.

3 Place the filter in the holder, then drop the holder into a second jar, with the holder's mouth pointing downward.

4 Gently layer the charcoal, sand, pebbles, dirt—even leaves from your garden—into the filter.

5 Pour the dirty water into the filter and watch the color as it flows into the jar. DO NOT DRINK THIS WATER!

What happened?

Your filter took out a lot of the gucky stuff. But the water is still not good to drink because tiny things like bacteria and viruses can get through the filter. Some places have very dirty water and people who drink it get very sick. The further away the water's source, the more likely it is to be polluted. If water comes from a river that is polluted upstream, it may carry fertilizer, chemicals, and waste from sewers and animals. People around the world are working to make water cleaner and safer for drinking.

How do oil spills hurt sea life ?

Oil doesn't mix with water, but sometimes it gets released into the ocean. Then what happens?

You need

- 2 bowls
- water
- feathers
- towel
- vegetable oil
- dishwashing liquid

Do this

1. Fill a small bowl with cool water.
   Quickly dip a feather in the water.
   Shake the feather. Does the water stick to the feather? Pat the feather dry with the towel.

2. Add a tablespoon of oil to the water. Dip the feather into the bowl to coat it with oil. Hold the feather up. Does it keep its shape? Pat the feather with a towel. Does the feather look as it did in step 1?

3. Fill a second bowl with water and dip the oily feather into it. Does the water clean the feather?

4. Gently mix a bit of dishwashing liquid into the water in the second bowl. Dip the oily feather into the bowl and rub it gently in the soapy water. Does the oil come off?

5. Mix the oil and water in the bowl. Can you think of a way to take out the oil?

What happened?

Feathers resist water. They keep birds warm and help them float. But when feathers get coated with oil, they absorb water; they get wet and heavy. Birds can die. Detergent can remove the oil and return the feathers to their natural condition.

Oil spills are a threat to birds and to all wildlife. Oil tankers, giant ships that carry oil, sometimes leak. The leaking oil pollutes the water. But even more oil pollution comes from the changed engine oil in cars. Used car oil should be recycled. It shouldn't go in the garbage or down the drain.

There are volunteer groups that rescue sea birds and animals caught in oil spills. Volunteers wash the animals to remove the oil, and care for them until they can be safely released.

What happens to things you put down the drain ?

The next time you pull the plug in your bathtub, watch as the water swirls down the drain. Where does it go and what happens when it gets there? Do you think the fish in the ocean will enjoy your favorite body scrub? Let's see.

You need

* large glass bowl, like a fish bowl—but please, no fish!
* liquid plant fertilizer or powdered fish food

Do this

1 This is not a fish-friendly activity, so please use an old fish bowl without the creatures. Wash the bowl and have an adult help you fill it with water.

2 With an adult to help, place the bowl on a flat surface in a bright, sunny spot near a window.

3 Sprinkle several tablespoons of fish food or plant fertilizer on the water. Let the bowl sit undisturbed for a week. What color is the water?

4 Add another tablespoon of fish or plant food to the bowl. Wait another week. What do you see now?

What happened

It may not be the scum of the universe, but you'll see a lot of gross green gunk in your bowl. This gunk is algae, a simple fast-growing plant-like life form that lives in water on nutrients from soap and waste. An excess of algae uses up the oxygen in the water and leaves fish without enough oxygen to live. Fish-eating animals and birds no longer have food. Other wildlife must move away, or die.

Just as water runs from rivers and streams into the oceans, the water from your drains at home and from the streets and sidewalks of your town flows into the ocean. And the water carries with it all the things that everyone has put there. As all these nasty things build up, they can cause fish to sicken and die. So be careful what you put down the drain. Don't use products that can harm the environment. Be sure the labels on your bubble bath and shampoo say they are biodegradable. Biodegradable means they will break down over time into chemicals that are safe for living things.

Rocks, Dirt, Sand

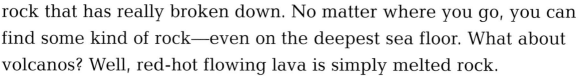

What's the oldest thing around your house? No, it's not your grandparents. There's something probably far older just beyond your front door. Go outside and look down. Do you see any dust? Dust is a rock that has really broken down. No matter where you go, you can find some kind of rock—even on the deepest sea floor. What about volcanos? Well, red-hot flowing lava is simply melted rock.

Pick up a rock and take a good look at it. Is it smooth or pointy? Squeeze it. Is it hard or soft? Drop it on the ground. Does it crack or break? Is it one color or many? Does it sparkle? All these things tell a story. No, not a bedtime story. They tell how rocks are formed.

We classify or sort rocks by how they are formed. Igneous rocks come from volcanos. Sedimentary rocks are compressed layers of sand deposited by water. Metamorphic rocks are one form of rock changed by heat or pressure into another. Wherever you live, you don't have to go far to find a rock. Concrete and cement are made from crushed rocks and glass is melted sand.

If you've ever built sand castles on the beach, you've seen that sand has tiny bits of rock and ground-up shells. Sand that's soft to walk on usually doesn't have many shells. Sharp sand that hurts your bare feet may have broken shells or coral in it. Black sand beaches, like those in Hawaii, have broken bits of lava from volcanos. The waves pounding on the shore break down the rocks and shells into tiny grains of sand.

If you look closely at sand, you'll see lots of black grains. Scientists have recently discovered that these grains, a magnetic material called magnetite, come from bacteria deep under the ocean. Just as we breathe oxygen, these microscopic life forms breathe iron. In the process of breathing, they produce magnetite.

In this section, you will learn a great deal more about the rocks in your everyday life. So get ready to rock on.

How do rocks become sand ?

Unlike ice, which is frozen water, rocks don't melt. But they do break down to become sand and, believe it or not, water is a part of that process. How can this be? Let's find out.

You need

* sand from the beach
* sand shovel
* adult helper

NOTE: MAKE SURE YOU WEAR SUN BLOCK AND THAT AN ADULT IS NEARBY WHEN YOU ARE CLOSE TO OR IN THE WATER. THE WAVES CAN BE DANGEROUS.

Do this

1. The next time you are at the beach, spend some time sifting through sand from different areas. Choose an area far away from the water, one 5 feet (2 m) from the water's edge, and one 3 feet (1 m) into the water.

2. Look for flat objects that appear frosted or clouded, perhaps in colors like blue, green, or brown.

What happened?

You found that sand is a lot more than just tiny sharp grains. Among other things, you probably saw many colored objects in the sand with frosty, etched surfaces. These are most likely bits of broken glass that have been worn and rounded by the tides. When water runs over hard materials like rocks and glass in rivers and streams, it breaks off tiny bits and erodes—or wears away—the material's surface, leaving it smoother. These tiny broken bits of rock and glass become part of the sand you see at the shore.

Temperature changes cause rocks to crack and break too, just as you may have seen pavement do on city streets.

What is under my feet ?

If you really want to get the dirt on soil, just go out and take a good hard look at it. It will open up a whole new world to you.

You need

* small metal garden shovel
* soft ground
* adult helper

Do this

1. Take a walk with an adult. If you're near a forest, river, or park, look for an area where the soil is exposed, like the side of a bank or a cliff. Can you see the different colors of earth? If you're in the city, look for a construction pit for a new building. The different soil layers are easy to see from the safety of the street.

2. Ask an adult to help you find a safe spot where you can dig a small hole. Use a shovel to dig just under the top layer of soil. What do you find?

3 Dig a little deeper, until the soil starts changing colors. What do you see now?

4 Now dig another layer. How deep did you have to go this time before the dirt changed colors?

What happened?

It may have surprised you to see that dirt comes in different colors. Just under the grass and twigs, the first layer was probably dark brown or black. This is the topsoil, a layer rich in nutrients deposited by earthworms and essential to plant life. The next layer may be a lighter brown color because of leaching, the removal of salts and minerals by water that has flowed through it. Below this may have been a reddish-brown layer, perhaps with tiny pebbles and gravel or larger rocks and stones. This is the subsoil. You probably didn't reach bedrock, the underlying rock layer.

Geologists are scientists who study rocks and soil. They can tell the age of the different layers of soil and rock and what the climate was like at the time each of them was formed.

How can I tell one rock from another

It can be very hard to tell one rock from another just by looking. But rocks are made of minerals, and you can tell minerals apart by their different properties. One mineral, pyrite, looks so much like gold, it's actually called "fool's gold." You can probably find good rock samples right in your own backyard. But how do you tell them apart? Here's a way to rate your rocks.

You need

- rocks
- resealable plastic bags
- paper
- pencil
- water
- soap
- iron nail
- penny
- sandpaper
- old dull butter knife

Do this

1 Take a walk with an adult and gather a number of rocks in plastic bags. Keep a record of where you find each one.

2. When you get home, rinse the rocks off in soapy water and let them dry. Put each rock back in the bag you used to collect it.

3. Take a sample rock and use it to try to scratch the iron nail, the penny, the sandpaper, and an old dull butter knife.

4. Try this test with each of the rocks you collected. Which rocks were able to scratch the most items? Which the least? Lay your rocks in order, from the fewest scratches made to the most.

What happened?

Some rocks were able to scratch every material, while others could scratch only one or two. Mineralogists, scientists who study rocks, determine the hardness of different rocks using similar techniques, as this is an important clue to a rock's identity.

A rock's color and surface texture (whether glassy or rough) also help identify it. Other identifying clues lie in whether the rock has crystals or grains, and whether it's solid or spongy or layered.

The hardest rock of all is a diamond. Only another diamond can scratch a diamond.

Environment

Now that you know a little more about the natural world, you understand how important it is to living things everywhere that you protect it. You can be a partner in saving the earth by practicing what are called the 3 R's: reduce, reuse, recycle. These simple good acts can help preserve the environment.

Reduce the amount of garbage you make. One way to do this is to buy items with less packaging. Another is not to buy things you don't need. You can make some things yourself, like greeting cards, wrapping paper, and picture frames, from stuff you already have at home. Read labels and buy things that are biodegradable.

Reuse items you have already. Take plastic or cloth bags with you when you buy groceries. Wash out plastic or glass containers and use them to store things.

Recycle paper, plastic, glass, and metal. If you have a recycling program in your area, use it. If you don't have one, write to your elected officials to see if you can start one. Try to buy recycled products, such as paper and plastics.

You know that lunch you take to school every day? It makes a lot more trash than you may realize. If you put those wrappers, juice boxes, and sandwich bags together with all your other trash for a year, did you know it might amount to as much as 1,000 pounds (450 kg)? That's what the average person throws out in a year. Simply taking a lunch with reusable plastic containers can reduce garbage, literally by tons.

Did You Know?

If you've ever been to a garbage dump or landfill, you've seen how huge an area it can cover. It can easily be 20 feet (6 m) deep and cover tens of acres. So what happens to all that stuff? Often, it just sits there. It may stay the same size, shape, and weight for 30 or 40 years, or even longer! Some landfills are eventually put to other uses; the mountains of garbage become parks or recreational areas. But think how much better it would be never to make the garbage in the first place.

How can I reduce garbage ?

What else can you do to help the environment? Did you ever think about saving up your garbage and using it? Probably not. It may sound pretty gross, but it's a good way to help the earth.

You need

* vegetable kitchen waste
* large pail with a lid
* shovel
* leaves or cut grass
* adult helper

Do this

1 Save your vegetable garbage, like banana peels, potato skins, and rotting tomatoes, in a pail. Do not save meat, bones, fat, cheese, milk, or anything else from animals. Do not save plastics, glass, or paper. Do not put kitty litter in the pail.

2 Have an adult help you choose an appropriate place to age the vegetable material in your yard or in a public gardening space. Make it a shady, sheltered area of dirt.

3 When the pail is about half full, take it out to your selected **compost** area. Spread out a shallow layer of the garbage.

4 Scatter leaves or grass over the garbage. Add another layer of garbage over this each time your pail is half full. Always top the pile with leaves or grass.

5 Sprinkle the compost lightly with water every few days. Don't soak the pile, just dampen it.

6 When the pile is about 3 feet (1 m) high, ask an adult helper to turn it with a shovel.

What happened?

Your saved-up garbage decayed, becoming food for bacteria and earthworms. These little creatures helped produce a nutrient-rich all-natural organic fertilizer for your garden. Spread this rich, dark fertilizer around your trees and flowers. It will feed them, protect their roots from heat and frost, and keep them from drying out, so you'll be able to use less water.

I'm just a kid!
How can I help the environment

How would it be to live without running water, electricity, heat, or air conditioning? Energy is needed for all these things and it comes from many sources: wind, water, the sun, and the burning of fuels. But we risk running out of some of these resources, and using some of them can pollute our air and water. So the less energy we use, the better—for now and for the future, for all of us. Here's one way to help.

You need
* bathtub　　* ruler　　* water　　* adult helper

Do this

1 Have an adult run a bath for you. NEVER PLAY IN THE TUB WITHOUT AN ADULT AROUND. Use a ruler to measure the depth of the bath water in the tub. How deep is it?

2 Next, drain the water and have an adult run a shower for you. Plug the drain so you can see how much water you used in your shower. How deep is the water after your shower?

What happened?

You might have expected otherwise, but you found that the shower used less water than the bath, meaning you saved both water and the energy to heat it.

You learned earlier that water has a cycle. One interesting effect of water's continual recycling is that there is as much water in the world today as there was millions of years ago. In fact, it's the same water. Molecules that dinosaurs drank could be in the very water from your faucet!

Did You Know?

How can everyone help save natural resources?

Here are some more simple ways you can save energy and water around your home.

1. Don't run tap water to get it cold. Instead, keep a jug of water in the fridge. It will always be cold and ready to drink. Add a slice of lemon for flavor.

2. Prevent drips and save water by turning off all the taps.

3. Wet your toothbrush, then turn off the water. You don't need to run water while brushing your teeth.

4. Use a bucket of water instead of a hose to help your parents wash their cars or to wash your bike.

5 Turn off lights, TVs, and radios when you aren't using them.

6 For short trips to school or the store, walk or ride your bike instead of taking the car.

7 Turn down the heat a couple of degrees in the winter and wear socks and a sweater if you're cold. In the summer, wear lighter clothes to keep cool and save on air conditioning.

SUPER SENSES

Senses

Where are you? How do you know? Look around. You are using the sense of sight. Now, close your eyes. What do you hear? A TV playing nearby? Car horns outside? With your eyes closed, your ears tell you what's going on and where you are. You can hear, another sense.

Sniff the air. Mmmm, someone's baking cookies. You know this because of your sense of smell. What's that on your arm? You don't need to look. Your sense of touch tells you it's the cold, wet nose of your dog, wondering why you are being so quiet.

You open your eyes and see a glass of milk. You take a drink. Ahhh, the milk is cool and creamy on your tongue. You can't wait to taste those cookies, too.

That was easy. You used your eyes, ears, nose, skin, and tongue— and you know where you are and what you are doing. But, where do senses come from?

Each one of us is made up of thousands of tiny **cells** that are too small to see. But groups of cells come together to make **tissues**, and when different kinds of tissues work together to do a job, they are called **organs**.

Certain organs in our bodies allow us to sense things about the world around us—to see, hear, touch, smell, and taste. They are called **sensory organs**. The messages they send to our brains are decoded so that we can do things—like catch a ball that someone throws (sight) or find the ice-cream truck (hearing).

Sight

Did you ever wake up at night in a dark room? If there's no light, you can't see anything. If there's some light, you can see a little—but things look different. You can't see colors.

Why does that happen? There are special cells at the back of your eyeballs—**rod** cells detect light and **cone** cells detect color. When there's only a little light, the rod cells take over. That's why you see only shapes, not colors.

Light is the secret to seeing. It bounces off objects and into the eye. Look at your eyes in a mirror. See the colored ring in each eye? That colored part of your eye is called the **iris**. The black dot in the middle is called the **pupil**. The pupil isn't really a dot, but a hole that lets the light go deep into the eye.

The iris protects the inside of the eye. If you look at a bright light, the iris makes the pupil smaller, so less light comes in. When it is dark, the iris opens up to let more light in the pupil.

Do you want to know more about the eye? Look here. When light enters the eye through the pupil, it goes through a watery pocket. At the other side, an elastic window called a **lens** stretches across the eyeball like a tiny drum. This lens not only bends the light, but it turns it upside down!

Finally, the light hits the **retina**, that layer of detector cells at the back of the eyeball that are shaped like rods and cones. When light hits the cells, they send a message to the brain through the **optic nerve**. Your eyes see the outside world upside down. When your brain receives the message, it turns everything right side up again—and what you see makes sense.

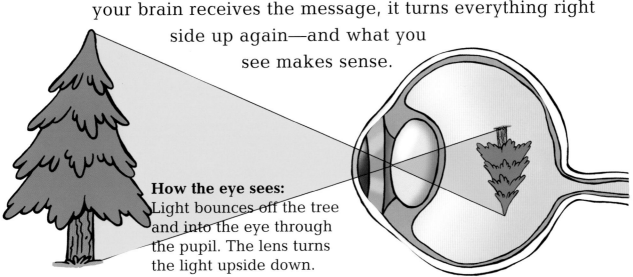

How the eye sees:
Light bounces off the tree and into the eye through the pupil. The lens turns the light upside down.

Why do some people wear glasses ?

You can't see inside your eyes, but let's do an experiment and find out what's going on.

You need

- adult helper
- clear drinking glass
- clear plastic wrap
- rubber band or tape
- water
- spoon
- a coin or small toy

Do this

1 Put the small toy or coin into the drinking glass.

2 Put a piece of clear wrap over the top of the glass. Fix it on with a rubber band or tape. The wrap should sag just a little.

3 Using the spoon, fill the plastic wrap "pocket" with water.

4 Look down through the water at the toy in the glass. Now, look at it through the side of the glass.

What happened?

The coin or toy looked bigger from the top. The water made an upside-down dome shape called a **convex** lens. Like the lens in your eye, your water lens bends light. It happens because light moves more slowly through water than through air. Look through a convex lens, like the side of a round fishbowl, and things look bigger. People wear eyeglasses with convex lenses to help them read. By bending the light, they bring the words on the page closer.

Sometimes people have trouble seeing far away. Their eyes don't **focus**, or adjust, from far to near. Everything looks fuzzy, so they wear eyeglasses to bring the world into focus, and see things more clearly.

What is a blind spot ?

Cover one eye with your hand. Can you still see, out of your other eye? Yes, but you aren't seeing everything. Remember those optic nerves that carry messages from your eyes? The place where they attach to your eyes is called a **blind spot**. Now let's see why.

You need

 the star and square picture below

Do this

1 Cover your left eye. With your head close to the book *look at the red star* with your *right* eye. (You should be able to see the blue square, too.)

★   ■

2 Keep looking at the star, and very slowly move your head away from the book. Stop when you can't see the square anymore. The book will be about 3 inches (7.5 cm) from the tip of your nose. (If you move your head farther away, you should be able to see the square again.)

3 Next, cover your right eye. With your head close to the book, this time *look at the blue square* with your *left* eye. (You should be able to see the star, too.)

4 Keep looking at the square, and very slowly move your head away from the book. Stop when you can't see the red star anymore.

What happened?

As you moved your head back, the blue square disappeared. After you changed eyes, the red star disappeared.

Each eyeball has a blind spot. Light bounces off the square and the star. It goes into the eye and hits the retina. But, that place on the retina is where the optic nerve connects. There's no room for the rod and the cone cells that detect the light—so nothing can be seen. In each eye, it's as if you were blind in just that one spot.

Can my eyes play other tricks on me ?

Sometimes the eyes and the brain can fool you. Your eyes may see something, but your brain doesn't. Let's take something as plain as the nose on your face—your nose. Look at your nose, right now. See it? Now, look down at your feet. Your nose disappears! You know it's still there on your face, but your brain ignores it.

Now it's your turn to trick your brain. You know all your colors, don't you? You can tell pink from blue? Let's see what happens when the colors are hidden in words.

You need

✦ this list of words

PINK   **YELLOW**   BLACK   **BLUE**   GRAY

GREEN   RED   **ORANGE**   PURPLE   **BROWN**

Do this

1 Look at the list of words, but *don't* read the words. Instead, say the *color* the words are printed in.

What happened?

I'll bet it was easy at first, but then you slowed down and began to make mistakes. It probably surprised you, because you know your colors. So, why did that happen? Your brain started to mix up the *color* of the word with the *meaning* of the word. Yes, reading the name of a color in a different color can get your poor brain so confused!

Did You Know? Crossing your eyes is good for you. The muscles that turn your eyeballs so you can see left, right, up, and down get a good workout when you cross your eyes.

Hearing

Is there a cat, dog, or horse nearby? Watch its ears and make a small noise. Don't you wish your ears could go up, down, and back and forth like that? Some people can "wiggle" their ears, but only a little. Human ears pretty much stay put, but they are shaped to capture sound out of the air.

Once the sounds enter the ear, they move down a tube-shaped opening called the **ear canal**. At the bottom, the sounds bounce off the **eardrum**. The eardrum vibrates, or shakes, and pushes three tiny bones inside your ear against a fluid-filled tube with hairlike detector cells. The sound messages travel from the sensors to your brain…and you hear!

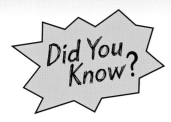

The three tiny bones in your ears that help you to hear have names. They are called the anvil, the hammer, and the stirrup, because that is what they look like.

The anvil looks like the big metal "T"-shape, called an anvil, that a blacksmith works on to make horseshoes. The hammer looks like a small hammer. And the stirrup looks like the part of a saddle that holds your foot when you're on a horse.

Now, here's a tip. If anyone should try to stump you by asking, "Of the 206 bones in the human body, which is the smallest?" answer "the stirrup," and you would be right!

If my eyes can fool me, can my ears fool me, too ?

When things are quiet—with no music or television playing—sit down, close your eyes, and just listen. What do you hear? A barking dog sounds very different from a closing door. But how hard is it to tell some sounds apart? Let's see.

You need

- ✳ a chair
- ✳ a helper
- ✳ sound-makers (see list)

Do this

1. Ask your helper to sit in the chair and listen. From behind the chair (out of sight), make some sounds from the following list or try some of your own. Ask your helper what you did to make the sound.

- ✔ rub your hands together
- ✔ tear a sheet of paper
- ✔ pour water into a bowl

- ✔ "slam" a book closed
- ✔ tap on a table
- ✔ run a finger along a comb
- ✔ shake a box of paper clips
- ✔ bounce a ball
- ✔ ring a bell
- ✔ step on some bubble wrap
- ✔ "pop" an air-filled paper bag
- ✔ knock down some blocks
- ✔ rub sandpaper against wood
- ✔ "plunk" a rubber band

What happened?

Did your helper get some wrong? Don't be surprised. Many sounds are a lot alike.

In movies, sounds like thunder and the wind are "made up." They're only **sound effects**. You expect to hear the sounds, so your mind believes the fake ones are real.

Take dinosaurs, for example. Dinosaurs lived so long ago, nobody really knows what they sounded like. Sound people, who work on movies, just make sounds up—and you really think you're hearing a dinosaur roar.

MEOW

Why do we have two ears ?

The game Marco Polo is usually played in a swimming pool. One person is "it" and moves around with eyes closed, calling out "Marco." The other players answer "Polo" so "it" can try to find and tag one of them. Two ears are a great help in this game. Why? Let's see.

You need

* a helper * a chair * a quiet room

Do this

1 Ask your helper to sit quietly with eyes closed and listen. Explain that you will make some sounds. Your helper should point toward the sounds you make.

2 First, move to one side of your helper. Softly clap your hands. Then, move quietly to the other side and clap again. Move farther away, to other places in the room. Clap each time. Is your helper following the sounds?

3 Now, ask your helper, with eyes still shut, to cover one ear tightly with a hand. Move around and clap softly again in several places. Watch where your helper points now.

4 Then ask your helper to change hands, and cover the other ear tightly. Again, move around the room and clap softly.

What happened?

When you were very close and your helper listened with both ears, he or she could probably tell where the sound was coming from. As you moved farther away and your helper listened with only one ear at a time, it was harder to find you. We can tell direction when we use both ears because of the difference in the sound coming into each ear. When we only hear through one ear, it becomes much more difficult to tell the location of the sound.

Why shouldn't I poke things in my ears ?

Did you know you have a set of drums? Not bongo, congo, or kettle drums, but eardrums. They're not good for pounding out a beat, but eardrums are great for hearing your favorite band—or a fire-engine siren.

Every sound you hear is caused by **vibrations** or waves. Your eardrums catch the sound waves that ride the air into your ears. This starts three very small bones in your ear vibrating, too. That's when hair-like detector cells in the ear, in a long tube called the **cochlea**, send the sound signals to your brain. Let's see how the eardrums do their work.

You need

* plastic garbage bag
* large metal bowl
* ruler
* crayon
* scissors
* masking tape
* salt

Do this

1. Lay the garbage bag flat on a table. Put the bowl upside down on top of the bag.

2. On the bag, draw a big circle about 2 inches (5 cm) out from the bowl. Cut out the circle you drew on the top layer.

3. Turn the bowl over and put the plastic circle over it. Tape it to the bowl, all around. Stretch the plastic a little to make it a "tight" drum.

4. Put a little salt in the middle of the plastic. Make loud noises near the drum and watch what happens to the salt.

What happened?

The salt moved! The top of your bowl drum vibrated, or shook. It detected sound waves—just like your eardrums do. But what if you made a hole in the bowl drum? It wouldn't work. Like a broken drum, your eardrums can be damaged, too. That's why you should never, ever, poke things in your ears. Your ears can even be hurt by loud noises—so you sometimes cover your ears with your hands to protect them.

Touch

What if you couldn't feel things? Even putting on eyeglasses or drinking water would be very hard to do.

You get your sense of touch from the skin. Your skin is the largest organ in your body. (Yes, it's made up of different kinds of cells working together, so it's an organ.) Skin is amazing. It is very thin, but it covers all of you—from your head to your toes. It moves any way you do, and it is waterproof. It's your first protection from the sun, dirt and germs, and other things that might hurt you.

Your skin is made up of two layers. The top part you see is called the **epidermis**. Underneath is a layer called the **dermis**. The dermis has sensor cells that detect pain, pressure, heat, and cold. They are always sending messages to your brain so you can figure out, "What *is* that touching me?"

Try this ➤ Sit down together with a friend and take off your shoes and socks. Now, gently tickle the bottoms of your friend's feet one at a time. Have your friend try the same thing on your feet. Did you both laugh when your feet were tickled? Now, try tickling your own feet. Did you laugh this time?

As it turns out, you can't tickle yourself. Scientists think that is because you not only know what's going to happen, you are in control of what is happening. So your brain tells your body that it is not being tickled.

Why do things feel hot and cold at the same time ?

Do you feel the bathtub water before you get in, to see if it's too hot or too cold? Sometimes, it feels fine on your hand, but too hot when you step in. That's strange. Did the water temperature change? What is going on? Let's see.

You need

* three deep bowls
* ice water
* warm water
* room temperature water

Do this

1 Fill a bowl half full of ice water. Fill another bowl half full of warm water. Fill a third bowl half full of room temperature water.

2 Place your left hand in the ice water and your right hand in the warm water. Count slowly to ten.

3 Take your hands out of the water and put them both in the bowl of room temperature water. Does the water temperature feel the same to both hands?

4 Try it again. This time place your right hand in the ice water and your left hand in the warm water. How does the room temperature water feel now?

What happened?

The room temperature water felt warm to the hand that had been in the ice water and cool to the hand that had been in the warm water.

Your skin cells can tell if they are "getting warmer" or "getting colder," but they can't measure the exact temperature. So when your feet are cold from standing on the cool bathroom floor, the bath water will feel "hotter" to your feet than it feels on your warmer hands, even though the temperature of the bath water doesn't change.

Can I tell what things are without seeing them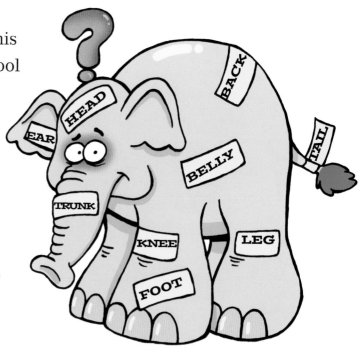

Did you hear the story about the blind men and the elephant? One blind man is holding the elephant's trunk. "An elephant is like a fire hose. Long and thick." The second man is feeling one of the elephant's legs. "No, it's like a tree trunk. Thick and bumpy." The third man is feeling the elephant's tail. "You're wrong. It's like a long rope with a tassel on the end." The moral of the story is, you can't always rely on just your sense of touch to tell you about the world you live in.

There isn't an elephant in this activity, but let's see if you can fool yourself and your friends.

You need
- ✱ 2 marbles
- ✱ 2 dice
- ✱ 2 cotton balls
- ✱ 2 lemons
- ✱ 2 each of other small things
- ✱ 2 small paper bags

Do this

1 Place one marble, one of the dice, one cotton ball, and one lemon into a paper bag. Place the other of the same object into another paper bag. (If you don't have two of each of these items, you can use two of any other small object that is safe to touch.)

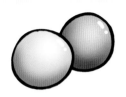

2 Reach your left hand into one bag and your right into the other bag. Without looking inside the bags, can you take out the two marbles?

3 Try to match up the other objects.

What happened?

You can match up the pairs because they feel the same. The marbles feel heavy, smooth, round, and hard. Nothing else feels like the marbles. Things have different weights and shapes, and feel different—hard, soft, smooth, bumpy, round, square. Each difference is a clue telling the skin on your fingertips what is the same and what is different.

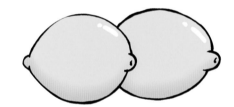

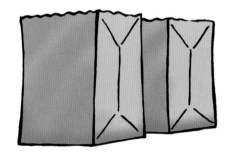

How do blind people read ?

Close your eyes and try to read the words on this page. You couldn't read a thing, could you? Blind people may not have the sense of sight, but they have learned to use other senses to tell them about the world around them.

You'd be surprised just how sensitive the tips of your fingers can be. They can even help you learn to read.

You need

* index cards
* soft surface (computer mouse pad)
* sharp pencil

Do this

1 Put an index card down on a mouse pad. Press down on the card with the tip of the pencil.

2 Turn the card over. Feel the bump? Put it aside.

3 Now, take another card, and make two bumps near each other.

4 Turn the card over and feel again. Can you feel two bumps, not one? If you can't feel two separate bumps, try again. Make the bumps just a little farther apart. Now feel them.

What happened?

You could easily feel one bump. That one bump is the letter **a** in **braille**, an alphabet used by people who can't see. When you made two bumps a little apart, your finger could "read" that there were two bumps. Two bumps this way **:** is **b** in braille, and two bumps this way •• is **c** in braille. The braille alphabet is made up of groups of bumps in place of letters.

⠗ = **r**

In braille ⠊   ⠉⠁⠝   ⠗⠑⠁⠙ means **I can read**.

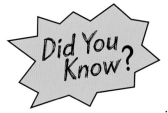
Did You Know?

Some elevator cars have braille numbers near the buttons for the floors. Next time you are in an elevator, practice reading the braille with your fingertips.

Smell

Take a close look at a bug. Can you see its nose? Some insects have over 100,000 hairs on their antenna and each hair acts like a tiny nose. The sense of smell is one we share with even the simplest types of animal.

Scientists think that people can tell the difference between about 10,000 different odors. This seems pretty amazing, but it isn't as impressive as the detecting ability of the family dog, who can identify over 20,000 different odors.

When you breathe in, tiny bits of things called **chemicals** that are floating in the air enter your nose, too. When these chemicals come in contact with detector cells high up in your nose, a signal is sent to your brain. Your brain allows you to figure out what you are smelling.

The group of cells that detect odor are only about the size of a small postage stamp and they are covered with a thin layer of **mucus**. If you get a cold, this mucus gets thicker so you usually can't smell very much.

The hairs in your nose are there to help the mucus keep out dust, flying bugs, and other small things.

Can I tell what something is just by smelling it ?

Stick out your tongue. Can you smell anything with it? If you were a snake or a Gila monster, your tongue would act as a nose and pick up smells from the air. You won't need your tongue, but you will need your nose for this next activity.

You need
* a helper
* 6 small plastic containers (not see-through)
* aluminum foil
* masking tape
* pencil and paper
* 6 different "smelly" things: banana, cinnamon stick, lemon or orange peel, whole cloves, coffee beans, garlic, mint leaves, pine needles, flowers, perfume, scented oils, spices.

Do this
1 Stick masking tape on each container. Write a different number, 1 to 6, on each container.

2 Ask your helper to put something smelly into each container and cover it with foil so you can't see it.

3 When you are ready for the test, poke 4 or 5 small holes in the foil cover. You can use the pencil.

4 Put your nose near the holes and sniff. Write down the number of the container and what you think is in it.

5 Take a few breaths of fresh air. This clears your nose of the first smell. Do the same with the other samples, taking fresh breaths in between.

What happened?

If the smell was strong and came through the holes, you were probably able to tell what was inside. Sometimes you think you know a smell, but you can't put a name to it. It smells sort of like…or almost like… something else. People can smell thousands of different odors, but that doesn't mean they can name them all. Being able to identify different smells takes some practice.

How do scratch-and-sniff stickers work ?

Do you like scratch-and-sniff stickers? You use your fingernail to scratch them gently and then you smell where you scratched. They smell much stronger after you scratch than before. Why is that?

Here are some ideas for making some scratch-and-sniff cards.

You need

- index cards
- pencil
- glue
- powdered spices such as cinnamon, onion, ginger, garlic, allspice

Do this

1 Print each spice name you will use on the back of a card.

2 Spread a thin layer of glue over the front of each card. Sprinkle some of the spice, that you printed on the back, over the glue. Shake off any extra spice that doesn't stick to the glue.

3 Let the glue dry completely. Scratch the spice and try smelling it. Can you tell which spice is which?

What happened?

When you scratched at the cards you made, some of the chemicals that give the spices their special odors floated into the air. This is exactly what happens with scratch-and-sniff stickers. The chemicals that make up the odors have been fixed onto the stickers. By scratching them, you release part of the chemicals. Once the chemical is in the air, it can enter your nose and be detected by those special cells in your nose when you sniff.

How good is my nose at smelling things ?

Some people who can see are **color blind**. They can't tell the difference between red and green, or other colors. Some people can hear, but are **tone deaf**. They can't tell the difference between different musical notes. Now for something really strange: there are people who are **odor blind** and can't tell the difference between certain smells.

Your nose may not be as good at detecting things as your pet pooch, but just how sensitive is it?

You need

* 8 glasses or cups
* measuring cup
* water
* vinegar
* eyedropper
* measuring spoons
* vanilla extract

Do this

1 Pour half a cup of water into each glass and add vinegar as shown.

x   1 drop   2 drops   4 drops   10 drops   ¼ teaspoon   ½ teaspoon   1 teaspoon

1   2   3   4   5   6   7   8

2 Starting with glass #1, sniff each glass until you can smell vinegar in the water. What number glass is it? How much vinegar is in that glass?

3 Empty the glasses. Do the experiment again, but this time use vanilla extract instead of vinegar.

What happened?

I'll bet you sniffed several glasses with vinegar in them before you could finally say, "Aha! I smell it!" When you did the same experiment using vanilla extract, you probably smelled it earlier. Vanilla extract has a stronger smell than vinegar, so it is easier for your nose to detect it, even if there is only a little bit there.

Taste

Y ou probably think most about taste when you are eating something very good…or so very bad that you run to wash your mouth out!

Stick out your tongue and take a close look at it in a mirror. Somewhere on that wet, pink thing are groups of cells called **taste buds**. It's these taste buds that tell you if something tastes salty, sweet, bitter, or sour. They also tell you other things about foods.

Maybe you like hot pizza, but think that cold, leftover pizza is gross. When taste and smell work together, you get something called **flavor**. The flavor of food includes how it feels in your mouth and the temperature of the food. When foods are hot, the smells are stronger. Your nose takes in these stronger odors, and your brain reacts to them. This is one reason why foods taste sweeter when they are warm than when they are cold.

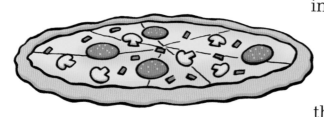

Is spicy a taste? If you happen to eat some food that has chili pepper or hot sauce in it, your lips might burn and your tongue would hurt. "Hot" or spicy foods cause the pain sensors in your mouth to send a message to your brain.

Chili peppers have something called **capsaicin** in them. When you eat them, or foods with the chilies in it, the capsaicin bothers the pain sensors in your mouth. The more chilies you eat, the hotter things taste! This is why, when you eat spicy foods, you think that your mouth is on fire.

But your brain gets really confused when you eat something with a strong minty flavor. It's "icy-hot," because your taste buds send both messages at once to your brain.

Did You Know?

There is something you can do if you don't like hot foods and your mouth starts to burn. Pop something without much taste—like plain bread, rice, or potatoes—into your mouth. It will take some of the "heat" away.

Where are my taste buds

The detector cells that tell you if something is sweet, salty, sour, or bitter are in your mouth. But where? And do they work on different tastes? Let's do some detective work.

You need

- a sink
- cotton-tipped swabs
- 3 small cups
- stirrers
- baking soda
- vinegar
- salt
- sugar
- water

Do this

1. Set up everything near a sink. Take some water and swish it around your mouth. You want your mouth to be nice and clean. Swallow or spit it out.

2. Dip a clean swab into some vinegar. Touch the swab to

your teeth and gums. Do you taste the vinegar? Now touch the tip of your tongue. Can you taste vinegar there? Try touching other places in your mouth and on your tongue. When you are finished, wash your mouth out with water until you can't taste the vinegar anymore.

3 Fill a small cup with water and add a teaspoon of salt. Stir until the salt dissolves. Dip a new swab into the salt water and test the places you did in step **2** . Rinse your mouth out.

4 Do the same as in step **3** again, but put in sugar instead of salt. Next, test the places in your mouth using baking soda.

What happened?

You found your taste buds. They are all on top of your tongue. You couldn't taste anything when you touched your teeth, gums, or other places in your mouth.

The chemicals that make up the foods we eat find their way to the taste buds hidden away on the tongue.

Try this➜ Go into the kitchen for some milk. Swish it around your mouth, then swallow and look at your tongue. Those little pink dots you see are the **papillae**, the little "caves" where the taste buds are hiding.

Why don't things taste the same when I have a cold

You sneeze a few times and your nose stuffs up. Suddenly, the things you eat don't taste the way they should. Maybe the cold germs are bothering your taste buds, too? Let's do a test.

You need

- *adult helper
- *lemon wedges
- *lime wedges
- *orange wedges
- *grapefruit wedges
- *pencil and paper

Do this

1. Close your eyes. Your helper will hold out small pieces of each fruit for you to smell.

2. Sniff each piece your helper holds near your nose. Can you tell what fruit it is just by the smell? Your helper will write down your guesses. How did you do?

3 After a moment's rest, close your eyes again. Gently pinch your nose closed, too, so you can't smell the fruit. This time, your helper will pass you pieces of fruit. Taste each one. (Remember to keep your eyes and nose closed.) Can you recognize the kind of fruit just from the taste?

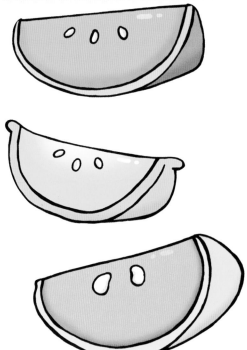

4 For the last part of the test, just close your eyes. Your helper will pass you the pieces of fruit again. You will be able to smell *and* taste it. What are the fruits now?

What happened?

Most people identify fruits from their smell. It is harder to tell what something is just from tasting it. Your sense of smell and your sense of taste work together as a team. When you pinch your nose closed, or a cold makes your nose all blocked up, food won't taste the same. But don't blame your taste buds: it's just that you can't smell it.

Can I taste color

What if you could change the way food looks? Would it still taste the same?

Ketchup is usually red. Now you can buy purple and green ketchup, too, but some people will only eat the red kind. Does changing the way food looks, change the way it tastes?

You need

- a helper
- colorless soda pop or white grape juice
- food coloring
- 5 clear drinking glasses
- spoon

Do this

1 Put some soda pop or juice into each drinking glass, about 1/4 full.

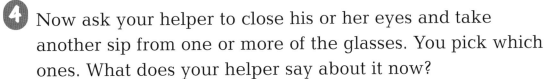

2 Add drops of coloring as shown, and mix well.

3 Line up the five glasses and ask your helper to be your "taste tester." Your helper should take a sip from each glass of pop or juice and tell you something about the taste of each one.

4 Now ask your helper to close his or her eyes and take another sip from one or more of the glasses. You pick which ones. What does your helper say about it now?

What happened?

At first, your taste tester probably thought the different colored liquids tasted…different! That's because we expect things that look different to taste different. Our mind just tricks us. You can't really taste colors— only flavors. Without seeing the soda or juice, your helper couldn't tell them apart.

WONDERFUL WEATHER

Weather

It's morning. You wake up and run to the window. Is it snowing or raining? Maybe it's sunny and hot so you can go swimming. Or, brrrr, it's very cold so you need to wear a heavy coat. Whatever's out there, that's weather. Weather happens. But where does weather come from?

Weather is the word we use to describe what's going on in the **atmosphere**, the pocket of air that surrounds our planet. Weather is what it's like now, or will be tomorrow. Look in the newspaper and see if you can find a chart that will tell you what the weather will be over the next 5 days. This is called a **forecast**.

Climate, another weather word, is not the same thing as weather. If you studied the weather over a long period of time for just one place, and recorded for many years what the weather was like each day, you would know the climate for this area.

Did You Know?

In a desert climate, like the Sahara in North Africa, it hardly ever rains. Animals and plants there have learned to live on very little water. There are no trees or grass for miles and miles, only sand and sky.

The climate is hot in the Amazon rain forest in Brazil, too, but it is wet all year-round. Plants there grow very tall. The plants grow so close together it's hard to take a walk through the forest. Sometimes you can't even see the sky.

Air and Temperature

When you talk about the weather, do you say, "It's cold" or "It's so hot today"? But how hot is it? A thermometer tells us how hot or cold the air is. The temperature goes up or down in steps called degrees (the symbol, °, means degrees).

Many places around the world use a **Celsius** thermometer. On this thermometer, water freezes at 0 degrees and boils at 100 degrees. A very hot day might have a temperature of 40 degrees Celsius, or 40°**C**. If it was -5 degrees Celsius, meaning 5 degrees lower than 0, you might go ice-skating outdoors.

Other places use a **Fahrenheit** scale to measure temperature. On a Fahrenheit thermometer, water boils at 212 degrees and freezes at 32 degrees. A very hot day would measure around 100 degrees Fahrenheit, or 100°**F**, and you could skate outdoors at about 20 degrees. Which scale is used where you live, Celsius or Fahrenheit?

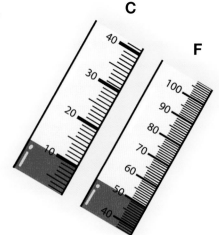

10°C = 50°F

Tip Keep the thermometer away from a hot stove or cold air when you are reading temperatures indoors. When you are reading temperatures outdoors, find some shade. The heat of the sunlight will make the temperature higher than it really is.

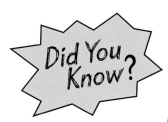

Alcohol is used in thermometers because it doesn't freeze as easily as other liquids. Red coloring makes it easier to see. Some thermometers use a liquid metal called **mercury**. It has a silvery look, but glass thermometers can break....and mercury is poisonous. So always be careful handling thermometers, and only use the kind with a red line in it.

How can I find out what the temperature is ?

Do you remember when you were sick and someone "took your temperature" to see if you had a fever? How do you take the air's temperature? Let's find out.

You need

* indoor/outdoor thermometer (with a red line in it)
* an adult helper
* a watch or clock

Do this

1. Find a thermometer. Be careful. Thermometers are often made of glass and can break. Always ask an adult for help in using one.

2. Hold the thermometer so the **bulb**, the round part, is at the bottom. Do not hold the thermometer by the bulb.

3 Turn the thermometer from side to side, level with your eyes, to find the red line.

4 What number is near the top of the red line? That's the temperature in degrees.

5 Take temperature readings in your room, in the kitchen, even in your bathroom (wait about 5 minutes each time). Have your helper run water from the cold and then hot water taps while you check their temperatures. Go outside and measure the temperature there.

What happened?

The red line may have moved up or down a little when you took the temperature indoors. The warm and cold water made it move more. The temperature outside was probably different from inside your home. If it was winter and cold outside, the line moved down. If it was summer and hot, the line moved up. But what makes a thermometer work?

Liquids **expand**, or take up more room, when they are heated. Very small bits of the liquid, called **molecules**, start to move faster. They need more room so they get farther apart. This pushes the liquid up the thermometer tube, the **stem**. When liquids get colder, they **contract**, or get smaller. The molecules slow down and come closer together. They take up less room, so the liquid slides back down the stem.

Is hot air the same as cold air ?

Liquids expand, or get bigger, when they get hotter. They contract, or get smaller again, as they cool down. Does air do that, too?

You need

* adult helper
* 10-inch (22.5 cm) balloon
* fabric measuring tape
* freezer
* watch or clock
* very warm tap water
* large sink
* baking sheet
* heavy pot

Do this

1 Ask your adult helper to blow up a balloon for you. (Balloons can be hard for kids to blow up. Do not put a balloon in your mouth as you chould choke.) Knot the opening to keep the air inside.

2 Wrap the measuring tape around the middle of the balloon. Write the measurement down.

3 Put the balloon in the freezer for about 5 minutes.

4 Take the balloon out and quickly measure it again. Write the measurement down.

5 Let the balloon warm up, then fill the sink with very warm tap water. Place the balloon in the water.

6 Cover the balloon with the baking sheet. Put the pot on top, to keep the balloon under the water. Wait 5 minutes.

7 Take the balloon out and measure it again.

What happened?

After being in the freezer, the balloon was smaller than when you first measured it. When the balloon was placed in the warm water, it got bigger. The air inside the balloon contracted, or got smaller, when it got colder and expanded, or swelled up, when it got warmer. Like the liquid inside a thermometer, air is made up of tiny particles called molecules. Warm air takes up more space than cool air because the air molecules move farther apart.

Why does my shirt sometimes stick to me on hot days

Have you ever stopped to look at air? "Don't be silly," I hear you say. "Air is invisible. You can't see it." Okay, but let's see if we can find something in the air.

You need

* a mirror with a frame or handle
* refrigerator

Do this

1 Put a mirror into your refrigerator for 10 minutes. Pick up the cold mirror by the frame or handle and bring it up close to your face.

2 Breathe hard onto the mirror.

What happened?

You couldn't see yourself in the mirror because it was fogged up. When you breathed out, **water vapor** moved out of your lungs, too. These molecules of water are so small you can't see them. But when your warm, wet breath hit the cold mirror, the water vapor turned into tiny drops of water. This change from water vapor to the mist on the mirror is called **condensation**.

There's always some water vapor in the air. It's called **humidity**. Sometimes the humidity is high (lots of water) or low (less water). On some hot summer days, the air is really full of water vapor. That's when your shirt feels sticky, and people say, "Whew, it's humid today!" Next time you are outside on a very cold winter day, huff and puff and see if you can "see your breath." That's water vapor!

Water

Water is a big part of weather. It comes down from the sky in the form of rain, snow, hail, or something in between. It's all part of a **water cycle**, a very important part of the world we live in.

Here's how it works. The heat from the sun warms up the Earth and everything on it. When you get out of a pool on a hot day and sit in the sun, the drops of water that cover your body soon disappear. The water has **evaporated**. This means the air has taken the water and turned it into water vapor.

Evaporation is happening all over the world. Water from lakes, oceans, rivers, streams, and even swimming pools is evaporating and moving into the air. The warm wet air moves upward and cools off. That's when clouds form. When there's enough water vapor in the clouds, or when the clouds turn colder, the water turns into drops and falls back to earth in the form of rain or snow. The water fills the lakes, streams, rivers and oceans... and it begins all over again.

Why is the grass wet, when it didn't rain last night ?

If you wake up early on warm summer days, you may find the grass and leaves covered with cold, wet drops of water. It didn't rain, so why are there water drops all over? This water is called **dew**, and it didn't fall from the sky. It's not magic either. It's science!

You need

* a warm day
* tin can with label removed (check for sharp edges)
* water
* crushed ice or ice cubes
* towel

Do this

1. Take the can outside on a warm day. Set it down where it is flat.

2 Fill the can halfway with water. Dry the outside of the can with a towel.

3 Add ice until the can is filled up. Watch what happens on the outside of the can.

What happened?

Tiny drops of water suddenly appeared. You made dew!

The warm air around the can had water vapor in it. When the air touched the sides of the cold can, it cooled down. This made the water vapor in the cooler air **condense**, turn into liquid, and made dew drops form on the can.

Where do clouds come from?

Look up in the sky. Do you see any clouds? What do
they look like? Some clouds are fluffy and white, like cotton balls.
Others are dark, almost black, and make you grab an umbrella. At
sunrise and sunset, clouds can look red, purple, or
yellow—as if they were colored with crayons.
But what are clouds anyway?

You can't reach out and touch the clouds,
but you can make your own in a bottle.

You need

- an adult helper
- a huge, empty glass jar
- metal strainer
- hot water
- ice cubes

Do this

1 Have your helper fill the jar with hot water,
leave it there for two minutes, then pour
out most of the water, leaving just an inch
or two at the bottom of the jar.

2 It's your turn now. Put the strainer over the mouth of the jar. Fill the strainer with ice cubes. Watch the jar.

What happened?

A cloud formed in the jar! Some of the hot water at the bottom of the jar turned into hot water vapor. The water vapor rose and bumped into the cold air coming off the ice cubes. When the water vapor condensed, it formed a cloud.

Hot air rises and carries with it lots of water vapor. The higher the air rises, the more it cools down. Soon the cold air can't hold all the water vapor so it starts turning into tiny water drops, and becomes a cloud.

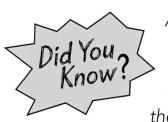

Did You Know?

A cloud's color depends on how much water vapor or drops are in it. Some clouds are white because sunlight goes straight through. Black or storm clouds have lots of big water drops in them, so light can't get through. That's why rain clouds sometimes look dark and scary.

Why is the sky blue?

When you first learned the names of the colors and looked up at the sky, the first question you probably asked was "Why is the sky blue?" What exactly gives the sky its color?

You've made a cloud in a bottle, now here's some blue sky in a glass.

You need

- a helper
- tall, thin glass
- water
- sheet of white paper or cardboard
- flashlight
- whole milk
- tablespoon

Do this

1 Fill a glass with water and place it on a table. Have a helper hold the sheet up behind the glass. (If you don't have a helper, you can prop the sheet up against something.)

2 Turn off all the lights in the room. Shine a flashlight through the water so that the light lands on the white sheet. What do you see there?

3 Add about a tablespoon (15 ml) of milk to the water and shine the light again. What do you see now?

What happened?

The light just went through the plain water onto the sheet. But, when you added milk, the water looked...blue! And the light on the sheet looked pink!

Even though light looks white, it is made up of several different colors. The blue color in light scatters the most, so the light bouncing off the fat molecules in milk looks blue. Red light doesn't scatter as much, so it went through the milk and looked pink, or reddish, on the paper.

The same thing that happened to your water when you added the milk happens to the sky. The light from the sun is scattered by small particles of dust or water vapor in the air, and this makes the sky look blue on a clear, sunny day.

Ice and Snow

Snowflakes are strange things: they are all the same but they are also all different. All snowflakes have six sides, no matter where, no matter when. But, because each snowflake is formed by different conditions, you will never find two that are exactly alike.

Why is that? Water molecules are shaped like triangles. When it's cold enough, and those triangles join together, they form **crystals** with six sides. How a snowflake grows depends on a lot of things: the temperature while it's growing, the amount of water in the air, and how long it takes to make the flake. So each one "grows up" to be just a little bit different.

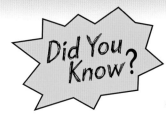

Did You Know?

Sleet is not hail; nor is it snow. It's like rain that couldn't decide what it wanted to be. Sleet can happen two ways. Sometimes rain falls through a layer of really cold air, so it freezes a little bit on the way down. Another way you get sleet is when falling snow melts a little on the way down, then re-freezes just before it hits the ground. No matter which way it becomes sleet, it's no fun to be caught outside in a sleet storm.

Did You Know?

On a clear, cold day, without a cloud in the sky, it can snow! It's called "diamond dust." Tiny ice crystals appear right out of the air. This only happens under very cold temperatures, when it's so cold even the tiniest bit of water vapor in the air condenses and immediately freezes.

Who made those ice pictures on my window ?

It's fun to wake up to ice pictures on your window. But where do they come from? And look, they're *inside* the window!

You find icy **frost** on your windows when it is *very* cold at night and the heat is on inside to keep you warm. But why wait for winter?

You need

- adult helper
- an empty, clean tin can
- crushed ice
- coarse salt (not table salt)
- water
- towel

Do this

1 Fill half the can with crushed ice.

2 Sprinkle a handful of coarse salt on top of the ice.

3 Add enough crushed ice on top of the salt to fill the can.

4 Pour about 1/2 cup (125 ml) of water into the can.

5 Wipe off the outside of the can with the towel, and put the dry can down on a flat surface.

6 Take a big breath of air and puff towards the can.

What happened?

You made frost! Your breath made ice patterns on the can.

The ice and salt inside the can made the outside of it *really* cold. The air in the room was warm, and your breath was even warmer. When the room air and your breath hit the can, the water vapor in the air got so cold so fast it turned into frost.

Frost "paints" patterns because snowflakes and frost are a lot alike. The water molecules that touch the icy-cold can are turned into ice crystals. The straight sides of the crystals join together to make patterns—like snowflakes—all over the window.

What is hail?

Have you ever been caught in a hailstorm? It's like someone in the clouds having a mini-snowball fight with you, but you can't throw back. Where do those hard, little ice-balls come from?

You need

- modeling clay (different colors)
- dental floss or thin wire
- helper

Do this

1 Pull off some modeling clay about the size of a jelly bean. Roll it in your hands until it's round like a small marble.

2 Take a larger piece of another color clay. Flatten it on a table or countertop into a circle. Wrap this clay circle around the clay marble piece so that it covers it completely. You should now have a clay ball the size of a larger marble.

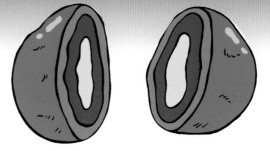

3 If you have other colors of clay, add a few more layers of different colors to the clay ball.

4 Use the piece of dental floss or wire to slice the ball in half. Look at the layers.

What happened?

See the different colored layers inside? Hail is made up of layers, too, but of frozen water. Rising air bounces falling raindrops back up into cold clouds. This turns the raindrops into tiny frozen balls—like that first ball of clay. The frozen balls begin to fall, but they get tossed back up again—like clothes going around in a laundry dryer. Coated with more water, they freeze again and again, until they are so heavy the air can't push them around anymore. That's when they fall to the ground as hard, icy hailstones.

Did You Know?

Hailstorms sometimes damage growing plants. Larger hailstones can weigh over 2 pounds (1 kg)—big enough to break car windshields and hurt people.
Hail is described according to size: from the small pea hail, to golf ball, and grapefruit-size hail.

Why is some snow fluffy and other snow soggy

Rain and snow both fall from the sky, but they are not the same either. Which would you rather shovel?

You need

- a straight, clear plastic glass or vase, over 5 inches (12.5 cm) tall
- crushed ice or snow
- measuring cup
- pen or pencil
- paper
- masking tape
- ruler

Do this

1 Stick masking tape up the outside of the glass, from bottom to top.

2 Starting from the bottom of the glass where the water would collect, make a mark every 1 inch (2.5 cm) until you reach the top of the glass. This is a rain gauge. (Put it outside when it rains. Empty it after you measure the amount of rain.)

3 Fill your gauge with 5 inches (12.5 cm) of crushed ice or snow and let it melt. Pour the water into the measuring cup. Write down how much water there is.

4 Now fill the gauge with 5 inches (12.5 cm) of water and pour it into the measuring cup. Write down the amount of water this time.

What happened

From all that snow or ice you only got a little bit of water. That's because water expands when it freezes. And fresh snow, like crushed ice, has a lot of air spaces in it. It takes 5 to 10 times as much snow to make 1 inch (2.5 cm) of rain.

When snow is very cold, it contains less liquid water so the snow is fluffy. It's hard to make snowballs from light fluffy snow. It's the wet water molecules that stick snowballs together. Soggy snow is much wetter. If you use your rain gauge on different kinds of snow, you'll see that soggy snow has much more water than snow that is fine and light. Shoveling really wet snow can make you feel as if you were shoveling rain.

Wind

What is wind? The simple answer is "air on the move." Wind speed is measured in miles or kilometers per hour (mph/kph), the same as speed is measured in cars. But at sea, sailors use the word "knots" (for nautical miles) per hour.

Want to know how fast the wind is blowing? Something called the **Beaufort scale** is used to measure wind. Here is a wind chart to help you tell how fast the wind is blowing.

Easy Wind Chart

1 Do you see smoke? Is it going straight up? Is the flag on a pole not moving at all? There's no wind. **0** mph = zero miles per hour (or **0** kph = zero kilometers per hour).

2 Is smoke drifting a little in one direction? Does it look like maybe the clouds are moving? There's some air movement, maybe **1** to **3** mph (**1** to **5** kph).

3 Can you feel the wind on your face? Can you hear tree leaves rustling? Is the flag moving on the pole? There's a little breeze, probably about **4** to **7** mph (**6** to **11** kph).

4 Now the leaves and small branches are moving more. Small, light flags are waving. Fluffy clouds are moving across the sky. The wind is going maybe **8** to **12** mph (**12** to **19** kph). If you like kites, it's a good time now to run and get it.

5 Dust and papers are blowing around. Smaller tree branches are swaying and flags are flapping in the breeze. The wind is probably about **13** to **18** mph (**20** to **28** kph). Hold onto that kite!

6 Now even small trees are swaying. The wind is moving about **19** to **24** mph (**29** to **38** kph). I hope you have a strong string on your kite.

7 Look! Even bigger tree branches are moving. Things are blowing all around. The wind must be going **25** to **31** mph (**39** to **50** kph)! Kite-flying is too dangerous. It's even hard to stand. We'd better go inside.

Where does wind come from ?

Wind can be wonderful. On hot summer days, a light breeze will cool you down. Wind scatters seeds so that new plants can take root and grow. What makes wind happen?

You need

* adult helper
* paper and pencil
* scissors
* thumbtack
* thread
* clothes hanger
* a heat source

Do this

1. On a piece of paper, have an adult help you draw a spiral shape, then cut it out.

2. Ask your helper to poke a small hole in the center of the spiral with the thumbtack.

3 Push one end of the thread through the hole in the spiral. Tie it. Then attach the other end to a middle of a clothes hanger.

4 Hold or hang the hanger with the spiral several inches above a radiator, a lit table lamp, or even a metal pan heated by the sun. (Don't put the spiral too close to the heat, and take it down when you are finished. Never leave it hanging near heat when you are not there to watch it.)

What happened?

The spiral moved! As the warm air moved upward, it pushed against the underside of the spiral, and made it spin.

It's this upward movement of air that causes winds. As warm air rises, the air pressure under it gets lower and cooler air nearby moves in to take its place. This sideways moving air is wind, and it usually brings a change in the weather.

Which way is the wind blowing ?

Sailors need to know wind direction to set their sails to catch the wind and turn their boats safely. Airplane pilots can get an extra "push" flying with the wind. But wind direction helps **meteorologists**, scientists who study the weather, track storms.

You need

* your pointer finger
* glass of water
* a compass

Do this

1. Stick your pointer finger in the water to wet it. Hold your finger up, and blow on your finger. Feel the coolness? Blow again, and look closely at your finger.

2. Now, set your compass down. Turn it so the needle inside is pointing north, toward the letter "N." Stand and face the direction the needle is pointing.

3 Wet your finger again and hold it up so the wind blows on it. When you are ready, read the direction off the compass.

What happened?

The side of the finger you, or the wind, blew on felt cooler. It dried faster, too.

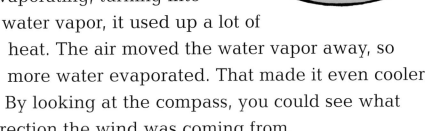

When the water started evaporating, turning into water vapor, it used up a lot of heat. The air moved the water vapor away, so more water evaporated. That made it even cooler. By looking at the compass, you could see what direction the wind was coming from.

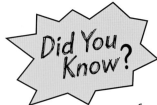

Did You Know?

Winds are named according to the direction they are coming from. A "north wind" moves from the north towards the south. A wind coming from in-between north and east is called a northeast wind ("nor-easter" for short). Around the world, winds can come from any direction: north, east, south, west; or northeast, northwest, southeast, or southwest.

What makes tornados go around ?

Did you ever flush a toilet just to watch the water go around and down? What has that got to do with tornados? Let's find out.

Note: Do this outside or at least over a sink because it can be messy. If you don't make a watertight seal, you could have a leaky tornado on your hands.

You need

* 2 large plastic pop bottles
* metal washer (to fit pop bottle opening)
* water
* food coloring
* glitter (optional)
* electrical tape

Do this

1 Fill a bottle about 3/4 full of water. Put a drop or two of food coloring in the water. (Add some glitter if you wish.)

2 Put the washer on the opening of the water-filled bottle. Turn the empty bottle upside down on top.

3 Wrap tape around two bottle openings, joining them together. Make sure it is *very* tight!

4 Slide one hand under the water-filled bottle. Put your other hand on the top bottle. Quickly, turn the joined bottles upside down. At the same time, move the joined bottles around in a circle a few times.

What happened?

You made a tornado! A funnel shape called a **vortex** appeared in the top bottle. That's because you moved the bottles in a circle. The vortex let a little bit of air rise up into the top bottle. At the same time, a little bit of water moved down into the bottom bottle...and the air and water kept changing places. The air spinning upward through the water is like the strong winds of a tornado, spinning upward into the sky.

Try the experiment again. Turn the bottles upside down, but this time *don't* move the bottles in a circle. Did you get a tornado?

Thunder and Lightning

Weather can be dangerous. Storms, with their thunder, lightning, strong winds and lots of rain can be scary and cause a lot of damage. When a bad storm is coming, the weather service issues warnings to give people time to get ready (board up windows and go to a safe place). You don't want to be caught outside in dangerous weather.

Did You Know?

Rain storms called **hurricanes** *have strong winds that circle around a low-pressure area. Meteorologists have a hurricane scale. It goes from a low of* **1**, *with winds from 74 to 95 mph (118 to153 kph), to a high of* **5**, *with wind speeds greater than 155 mph (250 kph).*

When Storms Come

1. Go inside or find some place to stay during the storm. Getting in a car can protect you from lightning.

2. Don't stand in the open, in a ball field or on a playground. Don't stand under a tree or another tall object. Lightning looks for the tallest thing to hit.

3. Keep away from anything made of metal: like poles, ball field seats, or fences. Lightning is attracted to metal.

4. Stay away from water. Get out of the swimming pool, or off a boat on a lake. It is not safe there. Opening an umbrella can keep off the rain, but it can't protect you from lightning.

5. Don't hold onto metal objects, not even a baseball bat or bike, if a lightning storm is *very* close. How do you know? It's close when the lightning and the thunder happen at *the same time.*

What makes lightning

Did you ever think clothes could help you with a science trick? Well, you may be shocked to find lightning there!

You need

- ✳ large mirror
- ✳ dark room
- ✳ nylon stockings, wool sweater, or silk scarf

Do this

1 Find a dark room with a mirror, and leave the light off.

2 Stand in front of the mirror, rub a nylon stocking together. What do you see in the mirror?

3 Do the same thing with a wool sweater or a silk scarf.

What happened?

Tiny sparks flew back and forth around the nylon stocking. It's **static electricity**. The sparks happen when **electrons**, tiny particles too small to see, move through the air. When lots of electrons build up in one place or on one thing, some will jump...and give off a static charge. This can happen when you take laundry out of the drier, or try to separate your socks.

On hot and humid days, lots of warm wet air sometimes moves upward very quickly. It forms clouds, and the temperature inside gets very cold. The very fast-moving air causes an electric **charge** to build up. The electricity builds up until the cloud can't hold it anymore. So it **discharges**, or moves out suddenly. That's when you get the bright "flash" of lightning and the "boom" that is thunder. Lightning is just one really big electrical discharge.

Did You Know?

The NASA website and some weather channels show lightning strikes around the world. It's hard to believe but, just while you were reading these few words, there were probably over 100 lightning flashes taking place somewhere on Earth!

What makes thunder ?

Thunderstorms can shake your house and make your dog run and hide. But what causes that loud "boom"? How about making your own thunder? It's not as loud, but you won't have to go out in a storm.

You need

⋆ a small paper bag   ⋆ a hard surface

Do this

1 Gather the opening of the paper bag together, like a little sack. Blow into the bag, then close the opening tightly to keep the air inside.

2 Smash the bottom of the bag against a table. Don't let go of the bag while you do this! Keep the air trapped inside. What did you hear? Was that thunder?

What happened?

When the bag "popped" open there was a loud noise. While this noise didn't rattle your windows, you did make mini-thunder. It happened because the air inside rushed out when the bag broke open.

In the clouds, the "boom" is caused by the sudden rush of air outward too, after being heated by the lightning flash. When a lightning storm is very near, sometimes you can hear a crackling sound—almost like the "tearing" sound of the paper bag—just before the loud boom or crash.

Lightning and thunder are a team. The bigger the lightning flash, the louder and longer the sound of thunder. They happen at the same time, but you always see the lightning before you hear the thunder. Why? Because light (the lightning) travels faster than sound (the thunder). They *seem* to happen at different times, but it's just that the light reaches your eyes before the sound reaches your ears.

Where do rainbows come from ?

If the sun shines right after a rain, look and you may be lucky enough to see a rainbow. But you don't need to wait for rain to see a rainbow. You can make your own.

You need

- a sunny day
- shallow glass baking dish
- a mirror
- water
- adult helper
- white paper or cardboard

Do this

1. Put the glass baking dish flat on the ground or a table.

2. Place the mirror in the dish. Lean it up against one side.

3. Turn the dish so the mirror faces the sun.

4. Add water until the dish is about half full.

5 Ask your helper to hold up the paper at the end of the dish away from the mirror and move it around slowly. Watch for the sunlight bouncing off the mirror.

What happened?

A rainbow appeared! The water in the dish bent the sunlight. Even though sunlight looks white, it has colors in it. And when the light is bent, it breaks up into red, orange, yellow, green, blue, indigo (a purplish color) and violet. This is called **refraction**. It's how white sunlight puts a rainbow on the paper.

After a rain, lots of small drops are still in the air. When sunlight hits the drops, the light bends to make a rainbow, just like the rainbow you made.

Did You Know?

Some people say there is a pot of gold at the end of a rainbow. Don't start off to find it, because you never will. Every time you move, your rainbow moves, too. The light that makes up the rainbow you see will shine through different water drops. That's why no two people can see the exact same rainbow; only their own personal one.

MIGHTY MACHINES

Machines

Wouldn't it be great if you had a machine to do all your chores? A machine that would clear the table after meals, rake the lawn, take out the trash—even pick up your toys. Maybe you'd like this machine to tidy your room, wash your clothes, or sweep the floor. Wait! This machine would do lots of the things that your parents do every day. Too bad we don't yet have a chore machine, but we do have a lot of other machines that make life easier.

Close your eyes and think of a machine. What comes to mind? Do you think of a sewing machine? Perhaps a monster truck. You probably didn't think about the wedge holding open the door to your room. This book will teach you about simple machines—machines that pretty much live up to their name.

Before you look at the machines themselves, let's think a little bit about the way things move and what makes them move the way they do. For instance, have you ever wondered why basketballs don't

float up into the air like balloons? While you may think this is a silly thing to ask in a book about machines, there's a good reason for this seemingly illogical question. The answer lies in the science of **physics**. Physicists study how **forces** like **gravity** act on everything in the universe, including those basketballs. For one thing, it's gravity that keeps basketballs returning to Earth after a good bounce. So let's get started by discussing some of the basic ideas in physics (see bolded words in Glossary, page 185).

Force Fields

Say you are in a swimming pool and you push against the side of the pool. What happens? The pool doesn't move, but you do. Now if you push against a shopping cart, you'll see that it will move, but you will not. In both cases you exert a force, but different things happen...or do they?

You can describe a force as a push or a pull. Forces work on objects that are moving and objects that are standing still. They can cause objects to move or change direction. They can also make moving objects stop. You can feel a force acting on you when you hold something heavy or you are in a car that stops suddenly.

When a force acts on an object, the object puts out an equal force in the opposite direction. That's why when you pushed on the side of the pool, you moved. But the shopping cart had wheels and you had feet, so it moved instead of you.

This is the effect of **friction**. Friction slows an object's speed of motion—by just how much depends on the **weight** (or mass) of the object and the surfaces involved. More mass, more friction; the reverse is also true. Smoother surface, less friction. A wheel, being smooth and round, reduces friction; feet in shoes cause more friction. Between you and the shopping cart, it's no contest.

So, why more mass, more friction? Because of another force called gravity. An object that has mass attracts other objects; it pulls them toward itself. How hard it pulls depends on the size of the object doing the pulling. Earth is enormous, so it pulls very hard; it has a huge force of gravity. Even though you may see balloons floating up and away, once the helium escapes them, they fall back to Earth.

How can I weigh really small things?

For the projects in this book, you need a scale to weigh things, but a bathroom scale doesn't really work. It's better to use what's called a spring scale. The easiest spring scale to find is the kind used for fishing. It works like this: to weigh something, like a small toy, just attach the toy to the hook on the scale and lift it up. The spring stretches and the arrow or marker points to the correct weight. But what if no one at your house fishes? You can always make your own spring scale.

You need

* rubber band   * paper clip
* ruler with a hole in one end
* weight from page 152 (plastic bag and rice)

Do this

1 Poke the rubber band through the hole in the ruler and pull one end of the rubber band through the other. Tug gently to make a big loop.

2 Straighten the paper clip, keeping the hook shapes at the ends. Put one hook through the looped rubber band.

3 Now weigh something: slip the other paper clip hook through a hole in the plastic bag filled with rice and let it hang down along the ruler. Note where the weight rests on the ruler.

4 Open the bag and remove some of the rice. Attach the weight to the paper clip again and see where it stops along the ruler.

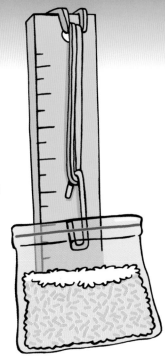

What happened?

You made a spring scale. The rubber band hanging down along the ruler acts like a spring and the marks on the ruler give you a rough idea of how much the thing weighs.

Simple Machines

Before you can understand how simple machines work, you need to know what work is. No, you don't have to get a job; you just have to know how scientists use the word "work." Work means moving a thing by pushing or pulling it over a distance.

A simple machine is a thing that makes work easier. It may have few—or even no—moving parts. You may think that machines have engines and lots of metal parts. Yes, a lot of them do, but don't be fooled. Even your front teeth are a kind of simple machine.

There are six basic types of simple machine: ramps, **screws**, and **wedges**, all belonging to a group called inclined planes. **Levers**, **wheels** and **axles**, and **pulleys** are members of the lever family. Any of these simple machines can make work easier by helping you move objects using less muscle.

Levers

Like you, levers belong to families sharing similar features. The feature that all levers share is a bar that balances or turns on a fixed base or pivot called a **fulcrum**. There are three families or classes of lever and each one has the fulcrum in a different place.

It's easy to picture a first-class lever; just look at a seesaw. The fulcrum is in the middle. A heavier person (the load) always moves downward and a lighter one (the effort) up. Move the heavier person toward the middle and the lighter one can lift the heavier. The closer the load to the fulcrum, the less the effort needed.

For a second-class lever, picture a nutcracker. The fulcrum is at one end (where the rods meet); the effort (your hand) is at the other. The nut (the load) is in between. If you've ever used a nutcracker, you know that it works best when the nut is closest to the fulcrum (the joint).

A toilet handle that you push down at one end is a third-class lever. The attached end is the fulcrum, the middle of the handle is the load, and your hand on the end is the effort.

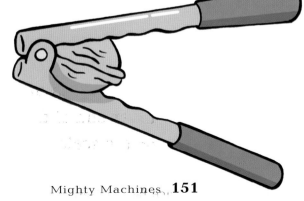

How do different levers work

Here's a simple way to see the three different classes of lever at work.

You need

- ✳ rice ✳ rubber band ✳ chair
- ✳ resealable plastic sandwich bag
- ✳ fish or spring scale (see page 148)
- ✳ measuring stick or wooden dowel
- ✳ adult helper

Do this

1 Make a weight: fill the plastic sandwich bag with rice and seal it. Place a rubber band around the bag and hang the weight by the rubber band.

2 Hold the stick steady across the back of the chair. Ask an adult to attach the weight to one end of the stick. Attach the fish scale to the other end of the stick. Pull down on the scale to lift the bag

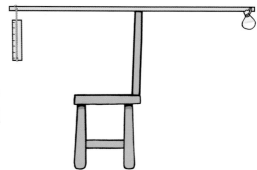

of rice at the other end. Have an adult help you read the scale. This is a first-class lever.

3 Move the stick so that only the end of it hangs over the chair back. Have an adult attach the weight to the middle of the stick. Use the fish scale to hold the stick level. What does the scale show now? This is a second-class lever.

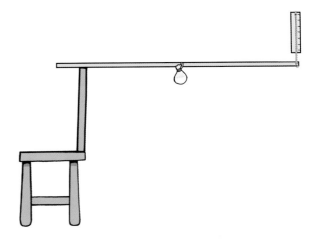

4 Have an adult move the weight to the end of the stick. Place the fish scale in the middle. Have a helper hold the end of the stick on the chair so it doesn't come up. Lift the scale until the stick is horizontal. This is a third-class lever.

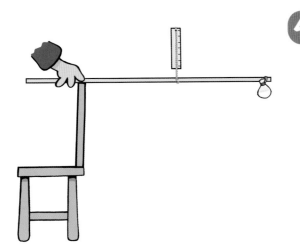

Can I use parts of my body as levers?

Do you like to play sports? Can you hit a softball out into left field or a slapshot in hockey? What do these games have to do with levers, anyway? Let's find out.

You need

- ✳ large, flat surface like a playground or backyard
- ✳ hockey stick or baseball bat ✳ measuring tape
- ✳ tennis ball or other small ball ✳ masking tape

Do this

1. Find a large, flat space, like an empty field. Use masking tape to make a big X on the ground. Place the ball on the X.

2. Put one hand at the top of the hockey stick, about 1 inch (2.5 cm) from the end. Place your other hand around the stick as far down as you can reach. Take aim at the ball and hit it. Measure how far the ball went.

3 Find the ball and place it back on the X. Move your bottom hand up a little on the stick or bat and hit the ball again. Did it go farther this time?

4 Keep hitting the ball as you move your hand up or down the hockey stick or baseball bat. How is it easiest to hit the ball? With your hands in which position did the ball travel farthest?

What happened?

Where you placed your hands changed the distance that the ball traveled. The hockey stick or baseball bat acts as a third-class lever. The ball is the load force at one end of the stick, your bottom hand provides the effort force in the middle, and the fulcrum is at the top, where your other hand stays still. When your bottom hand is closer to the ball, you can't hit the ball as hard—the distance between the effort and the load is too short. You have no *leverage*. As you move your hand up the stick or the bat, the distance grows and you can hit the ball farther.

Pulleys

What is the easiest way to lift something heavy? Just ask your older sister or brother for help, of course. That was painless. But what if that isn't an option? You can always use a pulley.

A pulley is a simple machine made by looping a cord or belt around a support. The support is usually one or more grooved wheels that turn smoothly and allow the belt or cord to move easily through or around them. Some pulleys move and are called movable pulleys. Others stay in one place; these are fixed pulleys. Often several pulleys are linked together to do more complex tasks.

Did You Know?

Over 2,000 years ago, a Greek scientist by the name of Archimedes was the first person to study the way levers work. He dared to boast that with a lever big enough, he could lift the world. What he

enough lever and someplace out in space to put the fulcrum, he could move the Earth. Archimedes is also famed for jumping out of the bathtub and running naked down the street yelling "Eureka!" ("I have found it!" in Greek) when he figured out the answer to another scientific puzzle. He was one smart but really strange dude.

Did You Know?

Historians believe that another Greek invented the first pulley. We barely know his name today, but Archytas, who lived about 2,400 years ago, invented several things we use every day, including the screw, the baby rattle, and the very first flying machine.

How can I lift up something really heavy

How do people move pianos and heavy furniture into tall buildings? It's easy if the thing fits inside the elevator or they can carry it up the stairs. If not, they might use a simple machine.

You need

- ★ empty thread spool
- ★ 2 chairs the same height
- ★ ribbon just thinner than the spool
- ★ 2 plastic pails with handles
- ★ string
- ★ broom
- ★ pennies or marbles

Do this

1 Run a piece of string about 1 foot (30 cm) long through the hole in the spool and tie the ends of the string together.

2 Slide the spool and string onto the broom handle. Rest the handle across the two chairs with the spool hanging between.

3 Put one pail on the floor and tie the end of a piece of ribbon to its handle.

4 Slide the other end of the ribbon over the spool and tie it to the handle of the other pail, which should dangle in the air.

5 Add a few pennies to the hanging pail. What happens to the pail on the ground?

6 Return the pail to the ground and add a handful of pennies or marbles. Pull the handle of the hanging pail toward the ground. What happens to the pail filled with weights?

What happened?

As you added pennies to the hanging pail, it started to lift up the pail on the ground. A single fixed pulley lets you pull in one direction to move a thing in the other direction. This is handy: it means you don't have to climb up a flagpole to raise the flag. Instead, you can stand safely on the ground and pull on the rope as the flag rises to the top.

Can I lift a weight with a pulley that moves?

In the last activity, you lifted a weight with a pulley that hung in place in the air. But how would it work if your pulley could move?

You need

- plastic pail with handle
- empty thread spool
- ribbon just thinner than the spool
- pennies or marbles
- string
- tape

Do this

1. Place some marbles or pennies in the pail. Lift the pail into the air and note how heavy it is.

2. Run a piece of string about 1 foot (30 cm) long through the hole in the spool, then through the pail handle. Tie the ends together.

3. Tape one end of the ribbon to the top of a table or counter near the edge. Since tape can leave a mark, ask an adult before you do this. If you can't use tape, have an adult or a friend hold the end of the ribbon on the table.

4. Run the ribbon underneath and through the groove in the spool.

5 Pull up gently on the ribbon until it lifts the pail. Does it seem lighter than when you just lifted the pail by itself?

What happened?

You made a movable pulley. In the last activity, the pulley was fixed: it stayed in place up near the broom handle. In this activity, the pulley moved as you pulled up on the ribbon. When you lifted the pail by itself, you didn't have to move your hand very far, but the pail was heavier. When you used the pulley, you needed to move your hand a little farther, but the pail seemed to weigh only half as much. With a movable pulley, the weight is distributed over, or supported by, all the belts (or ribbons). Your pulley had two supporting belts, one from the table to the pulley, and one from the pulley to your hand. This made the pail seem to weigh only half as much. And moving it seemed to be only half the work!

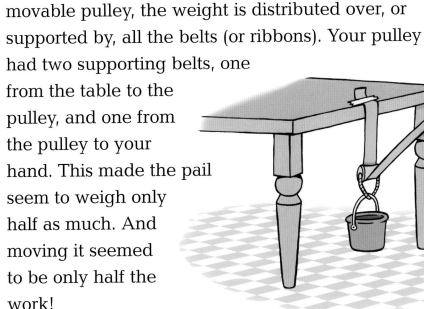

Wheels and Axles

It isn't known who invented the wheel, but the wheel by itself isn't much use. You have to attach something to it. Take a round candy with a hole in the middle and try to move something with it. You don't get very far, do you? Now place a thin pretzel in the hole as an axle and roll the candy around. This time you get somewhere. So a better question might be who invented the wheel and axle?

The wheel and axle is made from a large diameter disk (the wheel) and a smaller diameter shaft or rod (the axle). The outside edge of the wheel travels a much longer distance than the outside of the axle.

While you may know a "crank" as someone who is in a bad mood, there's another meaning for the word. A crank is a handle used to turn an axle. A peppermill uses an example of a crank. When you turn the handle, it turns the mill (axle) to grind the pepper.

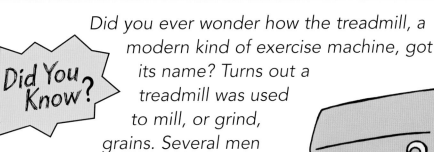

Did You Know?

Did you ever wonder how the treadmill, a modern kind of exercise machine, got its name? Turns out a treadmill was used to mill, or grind, grains. Several men would walk inside something resembling a "hamster wheel." As they walked, they turned the wheel, which was attached to an axle that went to a gear (a wheel with teeth) that turned the stone that ground the grain to make flour.

A yo-yo also acts like a wheel and axle, only with the yo-yo, the wheel is being turned by the axle. The string of the yo-yo isn't tied to the wheel directly; it's attached to the axle with a loop. When you pull on the string, it turns the axle in the middle of the toy that makes the wheel turn a greater distance. Then the wheel spins and makes the axle turn and the whole thing rises up the string into the air.

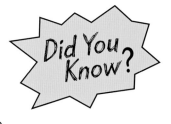

Did You Know?

Why do you need both a wheel and an axle?

A wheel is great for spinning around, but you'd have a hard time moving anything with a wheel alone. To move things with a wheel, you also need an axle.

You need

- 2 chairs with ladder backs
- broom handle
- string
- pail with handle
- masking tape
- safety scissors
- ruler

Do this

1. Place the chairs back to back, about 1 foot (30 cm) apart. Rest the broom handle across two level slats.

2. Tie a 1 foot (30 cm) length of string to the pail handle. Tape the free end of the string to the middle of the broom handle.

3. Place some pennies or marbles in the pail to make it heavier.

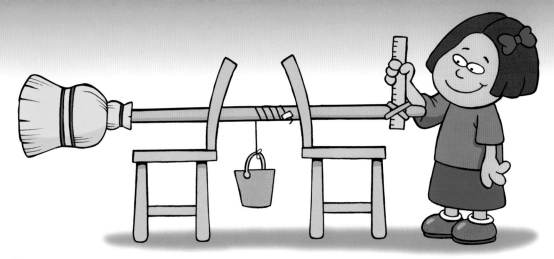

4 Turn the broom handle with your hands to raise the pail into the air. Turn it back the other way to return the pail to the ground.

5 Tape the ruler straight up and down on the broom handle near one end, as shown above.

6 Use the ruler, which acts as a wheel, to turn the broom handle and lift the pail.

What happened?

You lifted the pail either way, but it saved you effort in lifting the pail when you used the ruler (the wheel) to turn the broom handle (the axle). Your hand had to move further when you used the ruler, but the force you needed was less—the pail seemed lighter. The ruler acted as a bigger wheel, and the bigger the wheel, the easier it is to lift the load. And that is the purpose of a labor-saving device.

Why can't I put in a screw with my fingers?

One familiar tool you probably have somewhere at home is a screwdriver. This is another simple machine; it's based on the wheel and axle. Here's how it works.

You need

★ screw
★ screwdriver to fit the screw
★ piece of Styrofoam™ about 1 inch (2.5 cm) thick

Do this

1 Gently push the pointed end of the screw just a little way into the Styrofoam.

2 Try to turn the screw using only your fingers. Don't hammer it in with a heavy object. Does the screw go into the Styrofoam?

3 Now try to turn the screw with the screwdriver. Does it go into the Styrofoam now?

What happened?

You discovered why it's called a screwdriver. You found it was hard, maybe even impossible, to twist the screw in with just your fingers. But the screwdriver easily drove the screw into the Styrofoam. That's because the screwdriver and the screw act like a wheel and axle. The screwdriver (the wheel) is bigger around than the screw (the axle). You have to twist the handle of the screwdriver a greater distance to turn the screw a fairly short distance, but it doesn't take as much effort. Remember, the whole idea is to make the work easier.

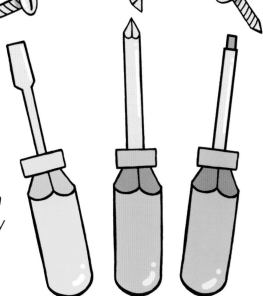

Did You Know?

There are many kinds of screwdrivers. A flat-head screwdriver has a flat top edge, a Phillips screwdriver has an X shape, and a Robertson has a square top. All these screwdrivers come in different sizes too, just like the screws they fasten. What kinds of screwdrivers do you have at home?

Inclined Planes

Inclined planes or ramps are something you see every day. They're often at the corners of city sidewalks, where they let wheelchairs move more easily off and on. Skateboarders do some awesome tricks off larger curved wooden ramps. And if you like to snowboard, you may someday try the huge half pipes, which are frozen ramps. Watch the winter Olympics or a TV show covering this sport and you'll see people fly!

Basically, a ramp or inclined plane is a sloping surface along which a load can be moved. The more gentle the slope, the more easily the load is moved, but the longer the distance.

An interesting thing about these simple machines is that, unlike pulleys, screws, and levers, inclined planes have no moving parts.

Did You Know?

The ancient Greeks told of a trickster king named Sisyphus (sis'-i-fus). Sisyphus tricked death, which angered the gods. As punishment, he was condemned forever to push a heavy rock up a hill (an inclined plane, by the way). As soon as the rock reached the top of the hill, it would roll right back down to the bottom again, and poor Sisyphus would have to start all over. Too bad he didn't know how to build a simple machine.

How did they build tall buildings ? before they had cranes

All over the world, ancient peoples built huge structures. There are the great pyramids of Egypt and equally impressive ones built by the Mayans in Mexico. But how did builders in these early cultures move the materials to the building site and lift them into place without modern construction equipment?

You need

* several large books
* spring scale   * small toy car or truck
* board about 18 inches (45 cm) long
* rice/plastic bag weight from page 152

Do this

1 Stack the books on the table near the table's edge. Lean the board on the table against the books to create a ramp.

2 Place the weight on the table against the bottom of the ramp. Use the spring scale to drag the weight up the ramp. Have an adult help you read the scale.

3 Place the weight on the table and lift it to the same height as in Step 2, using the spring scale. What does the scale read now?

4 Balance the weight atop a small toy car or truck. Use the spring scale to drag the weighted toy up the ramp. Was it easier to drag the weight on wheels?

5 Add or take away books to raise or lower the ramp. Does this change the effort you have to make to lift the weight?

What happened?

It was the same amount of work, but it was easier to drag the weight up the ramp than to lift it straight up. On wheels, the work is even easier, because the wheels reduce friction. The lower the stack of books (the more flat the ramp), the less force is needed to move the weight. A higher stack of books (a steeply sloping ramp) means you must use greater force to move the object.

Why are some ramps really long and others really short ?

If you've ever gone to an event in a large sports stadium, you may have walked up several levels of long, sloping ramps. Why do you think these ramps are designed this way?

You need

- board 4 feet (1.2 m) long
- several thick books
- rice/plastic bag weight (page 14)
- board 2 feet (60 cm) long
- fish or spring scale
- ruler

Do this

1. Stack the books so they reach a height of about 1 foot (30 cm).

2. Lean the short piece of wood against the stack of books to create a steep ramp.

3 Attach the scale to the weight and drag the weight up the ramp from the bottom. Ask an adult to help you read the scale.

4 Replace the short piece of wood with the long piece of wood and try the activity again. Was it easier this time or harder to drag the weight up the ramp?

What happened?

The weight reached the same height both times, but it was easier to drag the weight up the longer ramp than the shorter. You had to move the weight farther with the long ramp but it was easier. The shorter ramp took less time and distance, but it took greater effort.

In sports stadiums, many people have to move up and down the ramps. It is easier and faster for them to walk on long, gently sloping ramps than to walk up and down stairs or short, steep ramps.

Wedges

While wedges and inclined planes may look somewhat alike, these simple machines are used very differently. An inclined plane always stays in one place as objects move along its sloping surface. A wedge on the other hand is an inclined plane that moves.

A wedge often has two sides that slope or curve, while an inclined plane has only one. A wedge is pushed into objects to split them or to keep them from moving. A doorstop is a wedge; it's used to keep a door from banging shut. Axes split logs and knives cut vegetables, and both are wedges. Even your front teeth act as wedges when you bite into a carrot.

Wedges work because they are thin at one end and thicker at the other. You can feel that your upper front teeth curve from top to bottom; they are thinner at the bottom edge, where they penetrate the food. They become thicker toward the top, where they meet your gums. It's their shape that makes you able to pierce an apple and take off bites of a chewable size.

Most of the things used for cutting have a wedge shape. Axes, knives, and scissors are all wedges. One common thing you probably wouldn't even guess was a wedge is the zipper. When you look at a zipper, you see a row of "teeth" on either side of the fabric. To close a zipper, you run a slider along the sides of the metal or plastic edges (the teeth). Two wedge-shaped pieces inside the slider push the teeth together to lock the zipper. To open the zipper, the wedge shapes inside the slider pull the teeth apart.

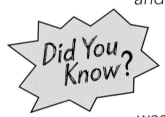

Did You Know?

How do wedges work?

Why do wedges have to be thin at one end and thicker at the other?
What difference does it make?

You need

* sharpened pencil
* new unsharpened pencil
* 1 inch (2.5 cm) thick piece of Styrofoam
* thick piece of corrugated cardboard

Do this

1 Try to push the end of the new unsharpened pencil into a piece of Styrofoam. Does it go in easily? Try this again with a piece of corrugated cardboard. Does the unsharpened pencil go into the cardboard?

2 Keeping your hands away from the surface, try to push the end of the sharpened pencil into the Styrofoam and then into the cardboard. Does the pencil go into the objects this time?

What happened?

When you used the pencil with the flat end, it was nearly impossible to pierce the cardboard or the Styrofoam. But the sharpened pencil could easily be driven into the objects. In fact, the harder you pushed the end of the pencil, the further it penetrated. The sharp end of the pencil is a wedge, just like the ones used to split logs. The wedge changes the direction of the force: you push down but the wedge pushes down and *sideways*, against the material on either side. This allows the sharpened pencil to move in or penetrate. The longer and narrower the wedge, the easier it is to push into something.

Screws

A screw looks kind of like a nail with rough edges. Instead of a smooth surface, a screw has a series of ridges along its sides. Though it may be hard to believe, this is another simple machine, and one you probably use every day.

Just grab a bottle of soda and undo the cap. Look at the inside of the cap and the outside of the bottle's mouth. See those lines? That's a kind of screw. Do you have a spiral slide at your playground? That's a kind of screw, too.

Screws are really useful for holding things in place. Push a cork into the mouth of a bottle, then try to pull it out. It's not that hard, is it? Now try to pull off the cap from a closed bottle of pop. You can't. The screw's ridges hold the cap tightly in place. So just what are screws and how do they work?

Try to imagine a screw as an inclined plane that winds around a shaft or rod with a wedge at the tip. The wedge is the pointed end. The inclined plane is the ridge (or thread) that wraps around the screw. So a screw is like a ramp that wraps around a nail.

Did You Know?

These devices all use screws.

Did You Know?

Remember Archimedes, the Greek scientist who liked to run naked through the streets (see page 157)? Well, not only did he explain how levers work, he also invented the Archimedes screw. This screw wasn't the metal kind you've been working with; it was designed to lift water from lakes or wells. In case you were wondering, Archimedes didn't name the screw after himself; someone else named it that in honor of him.

How do the ridges on screws work ?

You've seen earlier (on page 166) that you can't really put in a screw with just your fingers. You need a screwdriver (acting as a wheel or crank) to do the job. But it wasn't just the greater force applied by the screwdriver that drove in the screw. The ridges helped.

If you look closely at a screw, you'll see a raised spiral winding around its body. Trace this spiral from the pointed end of the screw to the top and you'll find that it's one long line, not a series of circles. What's the point of these ridges anyway?

You need
* screws of several different sizes
* screwdriver
* 1 inch (2.5 cm) thick piece of Styrofoam

Do this

1 Push the point of a screw into the Styrofoam and turn it in using the screwdriver. Note how easily it goes in.

2 Choose another screw with many more ridges and one about

the same length with fewer ridges. Use a screwdriver to turn the screws into the Styrofoam. Does it seem that some screws go in more easily than others?

What happened?

You discovered that the more ridges a screw has, the more easily it is driven into the Styrofoam. That's because screws with many ridges are like longer, more flat inclined planes; the ridges travel a greater distance but they make the work easier—the screw goes into the Styrofoam with less effort. When a screw has fewer ridges (its "ramp" has a steeper slope), you can screw it in faster but it takes a lot more effort. Pictured on this page are some common items you've seen many times. You might not have thought about it before, but they all work just the same way as a screw.

What would you get if you unraveled a screw?

Would you ever think that a staircase is anything like a screw? You might if you've ever seen a spiral staircase. You could climb one of these to get to the top of a tall building (it's like a screw with the ridges inside)...or you could walk miles up a gently sloping ramp.

You need

* unsharpened pencil with an eraser at the end
* 2 foot (60 cm) long piece of string
* thumbtack
* ruler
* helper

Do this

1 Push the thumbtack into the end of the eraser on the pencil.

2 Tie one end of the string around the thumbtack.

3 Hold the pencil upright on its unsharpened end and draw out the string so that the loose end reaches the table. Have a helper use a ruler to measure the distance from the pencil to the end of the string. Look at the string and pencil from the side. What shape does it form?

4 Hold the loose end of the string in one hand and rotate or spin the pencil. The string should begin to wind around the pencil in a spiral.

What happened?

The pencil with the string stretched out looked just like an inclined plane. And when you wound the string around the pencil, you had a screw! A screw is basically an inclined plane wrapped around a rod. Screws can go into very hard materials like wood or metal and they hold very securely. Just think about how small a screw is. If buildings had long ramps instead of staircases, the ramps might go on for miles.

Compound Machines

What happens when you put two or more simple machines together? You get a compound machine. Some examples of compound machines are a can opener (pictured here) and a construction crane.

The champion of compound machines was an artist named Rube Goldberg. He even inspired a Rube Goldberg contest where people try to come up with the strangest machine or most unlikely way to do a simple task.

Glossary

algae–simple, green, plantlike forms that generally live in water

axle–a rod connected to a wheel or on which a wheel turns

camouflage–coloring or markings used to blend into surroundings

caterpillar–wormlike early stage in the life of a moth or butterfly

cocoon–a hard shell or casing in which a moth or butterfly waits to mature

compost–decaying plant material used as fertilizer

condensation–the change from a gas to a liquid, or the liquid itself

evaporation–the change from a liquid to a gas or vapor

force–a push or pull that moves or alters the course of an object

friction–a force that slows the relative motion of objects against each other

fulcrum–the support on which a lever turns or moves

gear–a wheel with teeth that turns something else

grafting-attaching a bud or shoot from one plant to a similar growing plant on which the bud or shoot can grow into a mature plant

gravity–a force that pulls objects toward a body with great mass

lever–a bar moving about a fixed point called a fulcrum that allows an object at one point on the bar to be lifted by an effort exerted at a different point on the bar

molecule–the smallest particles that make up compounds like water or sugar

pheromones–chemicals given off by an animal as a signal to others of its kind

physics–the science dealing with the properties, changes, and interactions of objects and energy

pulley–a wheel with a groove that allows a belt to move a load

screw–machine with a grooved thread that fastens objects together

stomata–pores in leaves through which gases enter a plant

vapor–the gas form of a thing that can also be a solid or liquid

wedge–tapered object used to cut or split, or to hold a thing in place

weight–the force of gravity working on an object, as measured on a scale

wheel–a circular disk connected to an axle

Index